AF531426

Inter-Religion Marriages in Indian Society

Issues and Challenges

Arvinder A. Ansari
Mohini Anjum

The path to happiness is so narrow that two cannot walk on it unless they become one ...

L.G. PUBLISHERS DISTRIBUTORS

First Published, 2014

ISBN 978-81-910382-8-6

Published by
LG PUBLISHERS DISTRIBUTORS
49, Gali No. 14, Pratap Nagar
Mayur Vihar Phase I, Delhi 110 091
Tel: 011 2279 5641 email: lgpdist@gmail.com

Printed at
Mudrak, 30 A, Patparganj, Delhi 110 091

Acknowledgement

In a country which is so sensitive towards religious considerations, research in the field of inter-religion marriage was not an easy task. This book emerged from the major project sponsored by the University Grants Commission. Therefore, our first and foremost thanks is to the University Grants Commission for sponsoring the entire project and making this book possible. We would like to thank our colleagues at the Department of Sociology for all their encouragement at every stage of the project. We would also like to thank various offices of Jamia Millia Islamia for providing all the infrastructural facilities, support and cooperation during the entire period of the project. A host of others played an important role in this project, like most research projects, ethnographic or qualitative research is the type of venture in which the success of the project is heavily dependent on the cooperation of others. This is especially true of our respondents, who had to give so much of themselves to the researchers in order to understand their way of life. Without the cooperation of the couples, who were willing to put aside their fears and concerns and spent a considerable amount of time with us, endured the inconvenience of subsequent visits and telephone calls to seek clarification, this project simply would not have been possible. To them we extend our sincere gratitude. We would also like to thank the entire research team, in particular Shams, Gurpreet Shah Faisal, Uzma and Farheen. Their enthusiasm and insight prompted us to continue the study and learn more about such couples.

Additionally, we would like to thank a few scholars, particularly Prof. Imtiaz Ahmad, Prof. Tulsi Patel, Prof. Anand Kumar and Prof. T.K. Oommen as they are not only wonderful friends but reputed sociologists who helped us by providing insights into this population and offering their guidance in various ways. With their help, our understanding of inter-religion married couples was considerably enhanced. We would also like to thank the entire staff of the various libraries which we consulted and visited, especially Jamia Millia Islamia, University of Delhi, Jawaharlal Nehru University, Centre for Women's Development Studies and others for their assistance and invaluable help to trace books, articles and journals from various sources.

Finally, we would like to thank Adfar Rashid, Mirza Zeeshan Beg, Mrs. Sanjida Kirmani and Ms. Sanjida Begum for their contributions to the project in different forms and capacities. More recently, we owe a debt of thanks to Arvind Suri and Imtiaz Ansari for their insight and assistance.

Last but not the least we are grateful to our families for supporting us to work on the book using their precious time, first to work on the project and then to work on this manuscript. For those we have neglected or overlooked, please know you have our gratitude.

This study is only the beginning. We hope that more studies like this will lead to a better understanding of inter-religion marriages in India which will make the lives of such couples less taxing. The society will give them greater support in future and view such marriages as a step forward in the direction of secularizing Indian society.

Arvinder A. Ansari
Mohini Anjum

Preface

While appraising the available studies on mixed-marriages, either one comes across racial, ethnic or inter-regional marriages, studies reflecting that there has been a scholarly and academic disinterest in conducting the studies on inter-religion marriages, particularly in India. Hence, there is a substantial dearth of studies on such a significant theme in the sociological context. It will not be wrong to argue that such a marriage trend is deemed as against the normative social structure in India because of the subcontinent's cruel legacy of communal and violent history. Therefore, inter-religion marriages pose certain issues and challenges to the couples before and after entering their marriage.

Women bear the major brunt of it as experienced in the field. The anchoring question remains of the post-marital state of women who enter such a marriage and what is their pattern of adjustment in the newly embraced cultural, social and religious set up? What is their inner thought process? The worth-pondering and perhaps the worth-assessing aspect is whether there is a deeply embedded remorse or sense of guilt or pain of disconnection from their near and dear ones. Inter-religion marriages are always considered secretive if parents agree to it, what is the fate of their feeling of not being able to celebrate their marriages amidst their parents and relatives with the typical Indian pomp and show? The issues regarding the nature of treatment which is meted out to such women at in-laws' homes and issues of acceptance amongst in-laws keep surfacing in such marriages. Changes in religious behaviour with or without conversion are deeply scrutinized in inter-religion marriages. Do such women after conversion wholeheartedly follow the adopted religion or is there a superficial feeling of adherence to a new faith and the pain of losing their religious and cultural identity? There are the issues of conversion to survive and in case of no conversions, what remains the pattern of adjustment and 'being religious' of the spouses.

The challenging question which emerges, do such marriages lead to a secular ethos at home or is it merely a hypothetical myth? Is it arguable that such marriages are the idea of only secular minds and does really secularity emanate once the marriage is ceremonised? Or is it merely the intimacy factor characterised by contemporary job orientations, higher education and wider horizon of mindset due to mass media and outer exposure? Above all, romantic love affairs, etc., which though prompt couples to enter such unions but the same patriarchy prevails as an aftermath, disproving the secular nature of such marriages. Also how are social status, family background and occupational pattern related to inter-religion marriages is an area which needs to be explored. Besides, are inter-religion marriages always isogamous or is there any incompatibility between spouses?

Children, resulting from mixed marriages proved to be an interesting area of study. There was a beginning of the new generation which believed in spirituality and not religious superstitions. With children, parents also moulded themselves in new ideologies and belief systems.

This book answers the long due questions of conversion, assimilation and reconciliation. It is not an easy task to enter into an inter-religion marriage even when the portrayal of the time is modern, urban and global. There is over emphasis on preserving the culture. Similarly, the study also suffered limitations since people feared reliving those experiences or even feared to be recognised. To preserve the identity of respondents, we have used fictitious names. The study will reveal how, even in the twenty-first century, marriage by choice is looked upon as an insult to family and kin. It not only creates problems for the couple but also for immediate family members.

This study is an attempt to highlight the major problems that are posed in inter-religion marriages. It also tries to study the contemporary situation in urban cities from where all the respondents have been chosen. We hope to fill the void in academic studies with this book and also believe that this study will open the gateways for many such studies in future enriching academic literature.

Foreword

Inter-Religion Marriages in Indian Society: Issues and Challenges is a pioneering sociological work in an area which is sensitive and yet unexplored. The authors, Arvinder A. Ansari and Mohini Anjum have dared to tread a difficult path because they have chosen to study Hindu-Muslim marriages, the most difficult of all inter-religion marriages in India. All religious boundaries are difficult to tide over when it comes to marriages, but Hindu-Muslim barriers continue to be insurmountable and least acceptable by the vast majority of Indians. Even the highly educated and elite classes find it difficult to reconcile themselves to the idea of Hindu-Muslim marriages. The reasons for these attitudes against such marriages are varied and very complex. The memories of the history of 'Partition of India' and its aftermath continue to influence the minds of people even today and come in the way of reconciling Hindu-Muslim relations. The authors have studied the life experiences of couples in inter-religion marriages bring out a wide range of responses to such marriages by family, friends, neighbours and the society at large. Some of the couples have even suffered social boycott, ostracism and social exclusion because of their marriages.

The lived in experiences of both the authors accompanied by their deep insights and sociological imagination have enriched their data as well as their analysis. The in-depth study of all the couples in the sample brings out the complexity of relationships not only between the couples, their families and how they negotiate their cultural and religious differences, but also how they create space for themselves and their children in a socially and politically hostile environment. One of the most important strengths of the study is the multi-dimensional perspective adopted by the authors. The study covers a wide canvas in so far as it is a three-generational study. It studies not only the couples in Hindu-Muslim marriages but also their children and parents thus providing a wider perspective to understand the phenomenon of inter-religion marriages in India. The fears and tribulations of the couples for themselves, their children and their parents come out with great force and may leave a deep impact on the reader with a compelling need to reflect and empathise with such couples.

In a multi-cultural society like India, with its commitment to secular ideology and achievement of the new millennium goals, prejudices against inter-caste and inter-religion marriages appear misplaced. In a way, this study also questions the nation's efforts towards promoting secular values. Why is it that even after 65 years of independence, we have not been able to free ourselves of our social and religious biases? Can a country really achieve its promised goals with such deep-rooted prejudices? The book raises these very significant questions and provides the ground for further research in this area. At best, this could be seen as a starting point for a wide range of researches in a multi-cultural society like ours and compels us to introspect our own psyche. It should also be seen as an attempt to secularise a society trapped between traditional and modern forces. To some extent, the study also tries to unfold the impact of communalisation of Politics which fuels fundamentalist values that lead to communal hatred and violence and places such couples in inter-religious marriages at great risk-socially, physically and psychologically. The study highlights insipite of all barriers Inter-religion marriages are happening and are successful, it represents a new generation of more accepting individuals, thus strengthening nation's commitment to secularism, freedom and democracy.

Prof. Anand Kumar
Centre for the Study of Social System
Jawaharlal Nehru University, New Delhi

1

Introduction

A multicultural society is one with a plurality of cultures. It can take two forms. Cultures might be embedded in the lives of relevant communities. Such a society has a plurality of well-defined cultural communities; or its members might be drawn to different bodies of ideas and subscribe to them in different degrees without forming distinct communities. In either case, members of a multicultural society are not agreed upon common ways of understanding and organising their lives.

Today nearly all societies are multicultural. They consist of people of distinct cultures, holding differing views regarding family, companionship, the 'good life' and values for life and death. More and more countries are becoming culturally diverse; largely as a result of globalisation, technological changes, migration, etc. Diversity, however, poses some basic questions on a global scale, challenging social scientists, educationists and political leaders among others. What is meant by diversity of cultures? How are societies and nations to deal with this diversity? What attitudes are they to adopt towards it? How are culturally diverse people to live together?

India's cultural diversity has been a legend. It is the home of nearly all the religions of the world. The Indian Constitution recognises 23 official languages (including English and Hindi) and there are hundreds more spoken by over one million people. Its inhabitants include hundreds of tribes. It has no dominant or majority language. Followers of the Hindu religion do constitute a majority but, its largest religious minority, the Muslims, are equally diverse in nature.

India is a country which not only has multiple cultures but also multiple communities. The social stratification is based on various factors like caste culture, social status, economic status, etc. Even within the same culture, there are multiple communities which shows the composite character of the environment. There are thousands of communities in India which makes a close intricate web of social structure and culture. Within the Indian society, the institution of marriage is used to save one's cultural identity.

Marriage formed the strongest pillar of the values, virtues, faith and belief of any religion. It was not the union of two individuals but it was the approval of that union from the society which is essentially developed by religion and cultures. With marriage, an individual was assigned a definite role in the family that once again brought the joint family, kin group and religious practices in focus. In India, particularly since caste and religion are basic criteria in the selection of a mate in the kin-oriented choice, self-choice and love-matches are looked upon with complete disapproval.

It is important to first understand the definition of marriage with reference to the current discussion. Marriage is defined as a social institution under which a man and a woman establish their decision to live as husband and wife by legal commitments, religious ceremonies, and the community's sanction. India is a nation where each major city is a melting pot of different cultures. It is extremely critical to define culture as well. Culture refers to a shared system of meaning in terms of which people understand themselves and the world and organise their individual and collective lives. It includes views about the nature of the self, its relations to others, the individual's place in the world, the meaning and significance of human activities, relations and the human life in general, moral values and ideals, etc. It provides the framework, an intellectual and moral compass, in terms of which human beings navigate their way through life. A society's culture is embodied in its beliefs, practices, rituals, literature, moral vocabulary, proverbs, jokes, sense of humour, body language, and ways of organising different areas of life.

This culture accompanies the individual from birth to death in the forms of multiple rituals. Even if people move from their native places to big urban cities, the migration is not only a geographical or economic migration but a cultural migration as well. Marriage plays a very important part in the quest of conserving an individual's cultural identity. The phenomenon of inter-religious marriages challenges the conservation of the conditioned identity that we so very well accept in the name of culture. In the Indian context, mixed marriages are more about inter-caste and inter-religion marriages. In contrast, mixed marriages in Western society as a phenomenon are more about inter-racial marriages. We cannot deny that the challenges and issues concerned remain almost similar, that is of social acceptance and personal faith.

The society starts forming a layer around us from the time of birth to define our behavioural patterns. The first layer that surrounds us is of family. The family is influenced by religion which determines our culture as well. Therefore, an individual learns to eat, talk, and dress according to the community's sanction and society's approval. All the rituals that start from birth following us on our death bed are the product of religious and societal conditioning. It is assumed that in this particular situation, a conflict arises when people of two different backgrounds decide to spend their life together under the societal institution of marriage. The acceptance of inter-religious marriages is very rare and mostly limited to super elites. For a middle class urban family, inter-religion marriages is a matter of shame and for a rural society, it is a crime which has to be punished. The Indian upper class society still faces problems of acceptance in case of a mixed marriage. The marriage is further subjected to other sanctions. There are multiple questions which float on the relationship. Whose religion would be followed? What cultural values and norms would be followed? How would the children be named? Have the parents accepted the marriage? Even if the couple decides to live differently, the family values and norms keep haunting them. At the end of the day, it is the answers to the posed questions that decides the fate of the marriage.

Inter-religion marriages or marriage leaping over the barriers of religion reflect quite interestingly the degree of hold and continuity of the religious and secular values of life, having tremendous social and psychological impact resulting in wider institutional ramifications in the sphere of modernisation which are taking place. In the context of the ongoing process of industrialisation, modernisation and urbanisation, the frequency of inter-religious marriages is one reliable index of the genuine extent of the heterogeneity which is supposedly the outstanding characteristic of the modern urban social structure.

This phenomenon has a trendsetting significance in two ways. First, it contributes to pluralism, one of the distinctive features of modern industrial society. By pluralism, we mean a multitude of ethnic and other group of religions, beliefs and value systems. In the specific context of kinship and religion, inter-marriages are, therefore generally viewed as forces that create cosmopolitanism which in turn forms a typical pluralistic situation in today's social world. Secondly, in such a socio-cultural situation, different religions lose their ideological monopoly and various kinship structures exist side by side. As Karl Deutsch (1961: 494) defines, 'the social sphere of modernisation, where the major clusters of old social, economic and psychological commitments are eroded and broken and people become available for a new pattern of socialisation and behaviour'. It goes without saying that if the trend assumes a greater proportion, the consequential problem of assimilation will become a tremendous issue.

One of the factors mentioned most often to explain varying proportions of inter-religious marriages is that of religious distribution, e.g. the proportion of the total population which identifies itself with each religious group. The smaller the religious group relative to other groups, the larger is the tendency to marry outside the group. (J.L. Thomas, 1951). The modernisation process moreover promotes the assimilation of minority groups by eroding the importance of ascribed characteristics (Hirschmann 1983).

India and the West: A Comparison

Though the West has given acceptance to inter-religious marriages, but the fact remains that marriage between spouses of two diverse religions, takes place on a limited scale even in the USA. Mixed marriages are fairly common in USA—a plural and technological society par excellence. Nelson Lowry (1943) points out, inter-marriage in America has been gaining tremendous momentum in recent decades. Reiss (1972: 219) observes that 'despite the high degree of homogamy, we have a rising proportion of mixed marriages'. Williamson (1966: 257) comments that 'on a qualitative basis the inter-faith marriages looms somewhat larger than the inter-racial in American culture, but this depends on time and place'. On the whole, mixed marriages in the USA, according to Landis and Landis (1963), includes inter-sect, inter-community, as well as inter-racial marriages. If this extended or larger meaning of mixed marriages is accepted, it is safe to conclude that this phenomenon has a high frequency in the USA. Though there is less comparative data in other Western countries, there is every reason to believe that mixed marriages of this kind are on the increase there too, but its proportion may be less compared with the USA.

If this is the state of affairs in the most technologically advanced, industrial and secular society like the USA, it is not so amusing that in the traditional society of India, the phenomenon is almost rare. Such marriages do not get easy acceptance in traditional societies. Some of the inter-racial marriages also happen to be inter-religion marriages. But they cannot be considered as inter-religion marriages in the true sense, especially when they occur in a country like the USA where the problem of racism is a more real sociological problem than religion. So even when inter-religion marriages take place in the US, the issues involved more often are the issues of race rather than religion.

Larry D. Barnett's study (1963), 'Marriage and Family Living', on international and inter-racial marriages clearly shows that 'the rate at which native Anglo-Saxon Americans marry persons of a different nationality is unknown. But it seems that about two out of five members of minority nationality groups undertake a marriage with someone of a different nationality. The rate of inter-racial marriage varies by state, since many states prohibit inter-racial marriages. However, in 1959, California reported that 1.4 per cent of all marriages in the state were inter-racial.' She further states that 'there is some evidence that the rate of mixed nationality marriages is gradually increasing. A number of studies suggest that the rate of inter-racial marriage decreased in the first half of the century and prior to the 1954 Federal Supreme Court decision declaring it unconstitutional, segregated public schools. However, data from California indicated that the rate of inter-racial marriage has increased slightly since the court decision.

Rate of Inter-Marriages is usually studied in relation to particular religious communities in specific countries, like inter-religion marriages by Jews in the United States. The general conclusion of the studies conducted by Hoge (1995) and Ellman (1987) apparently suggest a rise in the rates of inter-religion marriages by Jews, as negative attitudes towards Jews have been falling slowly since the 1950s.

Some studies examine gender differentials in rates of inter-religion marriages, whether into or outside the group. In the US for instance, Jacobs and Labov (2002) examined gender differences in out-marriage rates among 16 racial and ethnic groups. Among most Asian American groups, they found that females were more likely to marry whites than males. As noted earlier, Merton (1941) found that among African Americans, men were more likely to marry whites than women.

Thus, the study clearly shows an increase in the number of inter-racial marriages in the US. Some of the findings of the study on cross nationality and cross racial marriages have brought out the following results—

1. Whites appear to be more willing to engage in inter-racial marriages with Orientals than with Africans.
2. Protestants have the highest rate of mixed nationality marriages and the Jews have the lowest, with Catholics standing between the two.
3. Apparently, among whites, it is the Protestant and Catholic males and the Jewish females who most frequently marry members of other races. In international marriages, it seems to be the Protestant and Catholic males who cross boundaries most frequently.
4. The religiously less- devout marry persons of different nationalities and races with a higher frequency than the religiously more-devout.
5. Those who have experienced disorganised and stressful parental families are more likely to marry members of other nationalities and races than those who were raised in cohesive and stable families.
6. People living in urban areas cross nationality and racial lines to a greater extent than those living in rural areas.
7. Persons crossing nationality lines to marry generally choose partners who are members of the same religion and of the same socio-economic level. In inter-racial marriages, the spouses generally come from different religions and apparently from different socio-economic levels. One study however, reports that the majority of spouses in inter-racial marriages come from the same socio-economic level.
8. Americans undertaking international marriages are usually from lower than average socio-economic homes. In inter-racial marriages, it appears that the non-white male has a higher than average socio-economic status and the white male and female and the non-white female have a lower than average socio-economic level. However, one study reports that the upper class is

highly over represented, and the lower class is slightly over represented in inter-racial marriages.

9. In African-white marriages, it is the African male who marries the white female in majority cases. In Oriental white marriages, generally the Chinese male marries the white female and the white male marries the Japanese female.
10. Among those who undertake an inter-racial marriage, a greater than average number have been married previously.
11. Foreign-born white males more than native white males, and native white females more than foreign-born white females, undertake African-white marriages.
12. In African-white marriages, the family of the African spouse seems to be more willing to accept the couple than does the family of the white spouses.
13. American males and females marrying out of their nationality or racial group are generally older than the average at the time of marriage.
14. The degree of success attained by international marriages is unknown. The evidence is contradictory regarding the success, in terms of divorce, of mixed racial marriages. One study found that such marriages between those of the same race, while a second study reported a failure rate for African-white which was not greater than average.

Even in a country like the US which is known for its democratic and secular values the above mentioned study shows that there is some kind of social ostracism, the cross racial couple in the US faces—

(a) Discrimination in the economic and business world—Not only may obtaining and holding a job be difficult, but career and mobility aspirations may become frustrating for both spouses. Securing the most desired housing often proves hard.

(b) Social ostracism—The couple may find its former friends and relatives breaking off relations with them,

> or an element of strain may be introduced into the relationships. Especially in African-white marriages, the white woman is often not considered as respectable.

An equivalent of hypogamous Hindu-Muslim marriage in India is found in African-American marriages, in the United States where a white woman is not often considered "respectable" after she marries an African. However, the difference between the inter-religion marriages in India and African-white marriages is that the children of such marriages are not a special problem. They are considered to be Africans, both by the white and African communities in the US. The identity crisis faced by children in an inter-religion marriage (Hindu-Muslim marriage in particular) has no parallel in the inter-racial marriages in the US.

In another study, 'Scientific Study of Religion' conducted by Paul J. Reiss (1965: 64), the author states that, 'it is possible, though improbable, that religious differentiation has been maintained at the same level in marriage, while declining in other areas. But it is hardly plausible that religious differentiation has increased without being reflected in a diminished rate of inter-faith marriage'. On the basis of the trend of inter-faith marriages involving Catholics (and also, by implication, most of those involving Protestants), we must conclude that there has been no major trend in the degree of religious segregation since the Second World War. The findings of the study reveal some similarity between inter-religion and inter-faith marriages involving marriages of Catholics and Protestants. These do not reflect any religious segregation in the US and the couples will continue to practise their own religion even after an inter-faith marriage of Catholics and Protestants. In India, in inter-religion marriages, especially among the educated elite class, the man and the woman involved either continue to practise their own religion or do not practise religion at all. But, in most middle class and lower middle-class families, conversion to the husband's religion takes place very often.

Globalisation has reinstated the concept of community identity or ethnic identity. Consequently, there are regional identities, asserting their cultural uniqueness and commonalities even within the most modern cities. The exposure to multiple cultures does not affect the caste-ridden societies, where rituals govern an individual from birth till death. This is the prime reason that in spite of the fact that we talk of the global village, traditional forces are very active. Owing to reinforcement of such values, people have become over conscious of their community identity. Therefore, some processes like secularism have been constantly under the threat of the rising tide of communalism and fundamentalism. To study inter-religion marriages in these contexts has become very important in modern complex societies.

The Indian story is somewhat different in terms of inter-religious marriages. The Indian social structure is undoubtedly a very complex institution. This social structure is 'essentially an inter-related system of caste, family and religion' Ghurye (1950:3). Consequently, marriage, religion and family are inextricably connected with one another in the Indian situation. Therefore, it is found that by and large the incidence of mixed and inter-religion marriages are of comparative rarity.

Current Academic Stand on Mixed Marriages

There has been a scholarly disinterest in conducting sociological studies on inter-religion marriages. While traversing the available literature, one comes across racial or ethnic studies being conducted in West on inter-marriages of people of diverse nationalities. It will not be wrong to argue that there is still a considerable dearth of studies on this theme. Sociological literature that is available on this theme forms one part of the wider universal process of social change. It is directly and indirectly related to all those works which theoretically and empirically deal with change in the institutions of marriage, family and religion in the modern society. Numerous American scholars have devoted their attention to inter-marriages. It was realised that its increasing incidence posed serious and some interesting problems related to the ethnic assimilation of USA from 1937, when Baber (1937) made his study on inter-marriages, till very recently, numerous authors have given us an insight into the structural and functional aspects of these marriages.

The book titled *Inter-marriage: Inter-faith, Inter-racial, Inter-ethnic* by Albert I. Gordon (1980), a trained sociologist brings 35 years of experience as a rabbi to this study of inter-faith, inter-ethnic and inter-racial marriages. His main hypothesis is that there will continue to be an increase in all forms of inter-marriages, and that no controls, such as waves of anti-Semitism, anti-Catholicism, or increased racial feeling will be sufficiently strong to stem it.

His second hypothesis was that inter-faith and inter-racial marriages are not likely to succeed, and that inter-religious marriages are a threat to the well-being of the individual, family, organised religion, and hence to society. In support of these theses, he marshals an impressive array of attitudes and opinions secured in personal interviews with official representatives of leading religious groups, with seventeen inter-married couples, and from questionnaires answered by 5,047 students in forty different colleges and universities. This original data is accompanied by facts and citations from empirical research and theoretical works of other social scientists, US Census data, and official religious documentary and historical materials. Dr Gordon states that the opinions of the students are 'what some college students think about inter-marriage' and is not a representative or random sample of all student opinion in each of the schools. He seeks to counteract possible unrepresentativeness through the use of a control group at North-Eastern University and the University of Hawaii. One wonders, nevertheless, if the results might have been different if the student sample had been random. The same question arises with reference to the religious officials and other specialists, such as psychiatrists, interviewed, and to 'people in major religious groups, as well as those who claim no religious affiliation'. Indeed, one might wonder how representative of religious, ethnic and racial inter-marriages are the seventeen cases which form an integral basis for some of his conclusions. Despite this possible methodological limitation, Dr Gordon's study is an updated comprehensive analysis of inter-marriage. Vividly presented are facts about seventeen inter-married couples who faced many of the personal problems implied in the main body of the study. The author separates his personal opinions, interpretations and recommendations from the factual and theoretical material. While the reviewer does not agree with most of Dr Gordon's personal views, she admires him not only for having the courage of his convictions, but also for his scholarly willingness, even eagerness, to stress the fact that his main convictions are diametrically opposed to the opinions and attitudes of the college students questioned, as well as much of the research reported by other social scientists. While Dr Gordon presents what he regards as incontrovertible evidence to establish his first thesis, his secondary theses are supported for the most part by his own opinions based on his experience.

Thomas P. Monahan (1973) in his paper titled, 'Some Dimensions of Inter-religious Marriages in Indiana, 1962-67' has dealt with the trends in inter-faith marriages. Data were selected from Indiana computer tapes, 1962-67, for detailed analysis of intra-faith as compared to inter-faith marriages for four religious groups – Protestant, Catholic, Jewish, other. The influence of age, previous marital status, and occupational class were examined, along with other factors such as age difference and type of ceremony. Although the proportion of mixed marriages among non-Protestants was found to be high and increasing somewhat, a comparison of actual with possible random mating disclosed considerable selectivity, with Jewish persons being by far the most endogamous and Catholics the most inter-married of the minority groups.

The paper titled, 'Patterns, Determinants and Implications of Inter-marriage among Arab Americans' by Andrzej Kulczycki and Arun Peter Lobo (2002), argues about the growing assimilation perspective. It argues that over eighty per cent of the US born Arabs and non-Arab spouses, implying a diminishing ethnic identification. The people with American education have a greater tendency to out marry because of the acculturation and structural assimilation, argues the paper. This paper is an effort to study the ethnic options for children of inter-married couples.

Another paper titled, 'Structural and Assimilationist Explanations of Asian American Inter-marriage' by Sean-Shong Hwang et.al. (1997), the authors emphasise two Inter-marriage perspectives. One explains Inter-marriage at the micro level and the other at the macro level, using individual attributes and other using aggregated community characteristics. This paper too points towards Inter-marriage as the offshoot of cultural assimilation. However it also treats sex ratio and group size as the other factor. This study provides information about the determinants of Inter-marriage for six different Asian subgroups residing in the US.

Yet another book titled, *The Decline in Marriages Among African Americans: Causes, Consequences and Policy Implications* (1995) by M. Belinda Tucker and Claudia focus upon implications of family formation among African Americans and towards the declining marriages. The author pointed towards the declining success of Inter-marriages among inter-racial marriages. The book covered ample discussions on social, historical and political issues that have shaped research on African-American families.

In India there is almost no work which exclusively deals with the problem of inter-religion marriages. However some notable scholars like Kannan (1963), Mokashi (1965), Newell (1963), Deshpande (1969) and Goswami (1972) have touched upon this topic peripherally.

Besides the above mentioned researches, a few more researches have been conducted in this area but these studies mostly dealt with differences in caste, region or culture. Some of these mixed marriages taken from the last two decades only, have been reviewed. There have been only two or three Indian studies on inter-religious marriages.

However the most recent study is an edited volume by Abdullahi-an-Naim's on *Inter-Religious Marriages among Muslim Societies*. It is a dense text which covers a rarely researched theme. The book is a collection of a few articles by different authors. Abdullahi has tried to present a picture of marriage between Muslims and others in cities like Mumbai, Senegal and Istanbul. The author brings forth such a complex process where social, cultural and religious identities are negotiated, not only at the societal level but at the individual level as well as and seldom at familial and community level. The book gives a basic contextual understanding and the role of actors (couples) in such marriages. The book also gives an insight about the social relations prevailing in our society. Abdullahi has touched almost all the basic themes that come under discussion while exploring inter-religion marriages like the comparative religious perspective, children's religious affiliations, gender and power within the family, marital stability, conversion, etc. The book has somehow described the phenomenon in a few cities globally.

Bambawale and Ramanamra (1981) studied mate selection in inter-religious marriages. This is very uncommon in India owing to the socio-cultural bonds of caste and religion, and tradition frowns on self-choice in marriage. Inter-religious marriages between Hindus, Muslims, and Christians are discussed in the light of socio-cultural, economic, socio-psychological, and ecological factors. The concept of love and its implications have been analysed. The factors which influenced mate selection were, character, common interest, personality, intelligence, physical beauty, sportsmanship, and position in society. One difference as pointed out in their study is that in America it is occupational propinquity and not residential propinquity of greater importance in mate selection. No single factor can be stated as solely responsible for mate selection, rather it is the result of multiple factors playing simultaneously.

In another study on the patterns of adjustment in inter-religious couples, Bambawale (1982) found that such couples have to make secular as well as religious adjustments. The size of the family, social status, cultural and educational background, and number of years of marriage are analysed. Adjustments had to be made in language, food habits, daily routine, social activities, and monetary dealings. These are all connected with the cultural and religious background of the family. Secular areas of adjustment have overtones of religious background. Each spouse had his own place of worship. There is no substantive evidence of tension due to religious differences.

In his study on socio-cultural and psychological implications of inter-religion-marriages, Cerroni-Long (1985) examines the influence of socio-cultural norms on endogamy and exogamy, with respect to marriage. It is suggested that the rationale of exogamy is the extension of a society's standing through creation of new links and alliances and renewal of old ones while that of endogamy is the maintenance of group boundaries for forbidding the introduction of outsiders in the kinship network and the reinforcement of intra-group ties and sense of identity.

In a research article titled, 'Gandhi and Hindu-Muslim Marriages' by L.N. Mittal (1999), which is in response to Ranjit Sau's article 'From Sankritisation to Hinduisation', it has been mentioned that Gandhi felt Hindu-Muslim inter-marriage are difficult. In a letter written on May 24, 1932 addressed to a lady, he said, 'boys and girls should be married only after they have grown up. The partners should choose each other with the consent of their parents. Hence there is no unnatural restriction in such a method. If anybody asks my opinion, I would say that marriage between those following different faiths was a risky experiment. If both husband and wife believe in their respective religions and actively follow them in their lives, difficulties are likely to arise between them. Thus I think that the Bhatia girl's marriage to Muslim boy is a risky step, but I do not regard it as irreligious. I would not oppose it if their love is pure, if the Bhatia girl can follow her religion and the Muslim youth his and if their ideas about food are the same.

But I do not advocate marriages between persons of different faiths as I advocate inter-caste marriages because I desire the disappearance of sub-castes. I would not agitate against such marriages either. This is an issue on which every man and woman should think and decide for him or herself. There cannot be a uniform law for all'. (*The Collected Works of Mahatma Gandhi*).

Ravinder Kaur (2004) engages in a very significant dicussion through her paper 'Across-Region Marriages: Poverty, Female Migration and the Sex Ratio'. It takes a dig at inter-regional marriages and documents and analyses an unusual response to the shortage of marriageable girls in the north. The need for women, for productive and reproductive purposes, is being addressed through unconventional marriages that are uniting rural, illiterate Indians across boundaries of region, language, religion and even caste. On contextualising across-region marriages, the average Indian marriage, especially in rural areas, is still perceived as governed by traditional rules of caste and community. These are rules of endogamy (marriage within one's own caste group although outside one's own gotra or clan), hierarchy (bride givers are inferior to bride-takers) and hypergamy (the woman must marry up, both socially and economically). The rule of caste endogamy is shared all over India. However, within the caste, isogamous (spouses of equal status) or hypergamous (spouses of unequal status) marriages may occur. In many parts of the north, village exogamy is another rule, making it imperative for spouses to be from different villages. Dowry, since it has become near universal in the country, can be considered as another rule. According to high caste customs, an honourable marriage is one accompanied by dowry and not by bride price (where the groom pays a sum of money to the bride's parents).

Parveez Mody's book titled *Intimate State on Love Marriages and Law in Delhi*, (2008) gives a clear indication of how secular vision in Delhi is the order of the day and how law, publicity and kinship along with community codes and established norms are now crossed over by youth which otherwise had a staunch ground especially in north India. Mody's book widens our vision to see and think about the prevailing intimacy among people and opens a new way of thinking on such issues. Love marriages crossing religious boundaries and defying community order is leading to a liberal citizenship. She has amply discussed the aspects of domesticity and publicity as well and also the rupture of the colonial period laws.

Rodrigues (1990) study 'A Comparative Study between Inter and Intra-religious Married Couples' shows that marriages across religions were more stable than marriages within the community and the reasons cited were that in such cases the entire responsibility of making the marriage a success was on the couple. With very little support from the family, the couples have had to put in more effort to not only making their marriage a success but also to prove to the world that their decision was a right decision and that they could make a success of their marriage in spite of lack of support from the families. Some studies on inter-caste marriages have also shown that both hypergamous and hypogamous marriages are as stable or unstable as compared to marriages within the caste. Hypergamous marriages, i.e. where the male belongs to a higher caste, the female belongs to a lower caste is a preferential form of marriage.

Inter-religion marriages have been the least researched area in sociology and social anthropology as access to data is very difficult and also because of the sensitivity of the subject concerned.There was a vacuum which was created on the issue of addressing mixed marriages. It is a difficult area of study especially when it comes to Hindu-Muslim marriages and explore the implications, relationships, problems of getting married, the marriage itself, its impact on the families of the husband and wife in question, the impact of such marriages on children and experiences of the couple, their parents and their children.

None of these studies have tried to show or find the impact of such marriages on the parents of the couple nor has much attention been paid to the children of such couples. Most of the studies in the US are concerned with the question of whether or not inter-racial marriages are more or less stable than marriages within the race.

Our study has focused its attention not only on the couples and their decision to get married in spite of differences in religious background but also see how the marriage impacts on the lives of the parents and the children, how they adjust to each other, to the families and to the society at large in spite of minimal or no support from their parents. The study is, therefore expected to go into depth and complexities of relationships that emerge out of the inter-religious marriages.

Law, Religion and Accepted Norms

India is a secular country and the Constitution of India gives every individual the right to practise any religion. Secularism also implies that one should respect the religion of others and not come in the way of the religious practices of others, i.e. one should not obstruct others from practising their religion. Although inter-caste and inter-religious marriages have always taken place in India, before 1954 it was very difficult for individuals of different religions to get married to each other. If they wanted to get married, one of the parties had to convert to the religion of the other. The mixed religious marriages historically have been an ideological dilemma as well as a threat to the different religious groups. It has been a dilemma because each religion espouses the doctrine of brotherly love and acceptance of others. But such a doctrine, when carried to its logical conclusion of marriages creates a peculiar situation. The abandoning of one's religious faith, in order to accept another in marriage, constitutes a threat to the organised religious bodies, since it means an eventual loss of followers. The couple attempt to resolve their differences over religion by one of the spouses accepting the faith of the other, usually before the marriage ceremony. Thus, an important characteristic of inter-religion marriages is the phenomenon of conversion and the loss of religious identity for that partner.

Inter-religion marriages are mostly personal choices. This is not only a phenomenon of modern times. St. Paul in the first century refers to inter-religion marriages in the Bible, when he exhorts Christians to keep their non-Christian partners (1 Cor. 7:12-13).

'If any brother has a wife who is an unbeliever, and she consents to live with him, he should not divorce her. If any woman has a husband who is an unbeliever, and he consents to live with her, she should not divorce him.'

To understand the attitudes and policies of the Roman Catholic Church towards mixed marriages, it is necessary to see clearly the Catholic conception of the nature and purpose of marriage. Marriage, according to Roman Catholics, is divine in origin, whatever additional human aspects and purposes there may be. It is intended by the creator to perpetuate the creative act and to beget children of God. Other ends, such as mutual helpfulness and love, are secondary.

The Muslim law of marriage ordains that the confession of Islam by the husband is one of the conditions for all marriages. A Muslim male, however, is allowed to marry a 'scriptural woman' (a Christian or Jewish woman) but not an idolatress, i.e. a non-Christian polytheist, Hindu, Sikh women, etc. Although the union with such outsiders might be valid if the conversion has taken place. However, Muslim women are prohibited by Islamic law from marrying outside the religion. Marriage between a Muslim woman and a non-Muslim man is possible only if he accepts Islam completely, boycotts all other faiths and believes only in what Allah says and what is written in the Quran. The purpose of conversion is for the acceptance of Islam wholeheartedly and not only for the sake of marriage.

The Sikh marriage ceremony is spiritual, religious, and a promise with God. When the bride and groom get married in the Gurdwara Sahib (Sikh place of worship), they do not only make a promise to help, protect and support each other but they also promise God to lead a spiritual life and to be one with God. This is why, unless the person believes in Sikhism, and follows Sikh beliefs, they should not get married in the Gurdwara Sahib. Inter-faith marriages are discouraged because they diluted the Sikh Code of Conduct to accommodate the wishes of individuals rather than following the Guru's teachings. In response, Sri Akaal Takhat Sahib—the Supreme seat of authority of the Sikhs—issued a *Hukumnama* (decree) regarding this matter on August 16, 2007 stating that the Sikh marriage ceremony should only be conducted when both bride and groom are Sikhs (as a respect for the Sikh religion). If the couple or either one of them is not a Sikh, then they must embrace the Sikh faith. This includes that they must change their last name to Singh or Kaur officially before the marriage ceremony.

The literature on Hindu marriages in India does not speak of inter-religion marriages per se, but rather of caste endogamy and inter-caste marriages as taboo. Moral and legal prescriptions for Hindu marriages can be found in the Dharmashastras. Out-of-community marriages were not uncommon in Hindu mythology and culture. In ancient India, there was the concept of *Gandharva Vivaha* which was marriage through mutual consent in the presence of God. No human being was required for approval of marriage. Some of these marriages were even glorified in the ancient texts. Dushyanta married Shakuntala, outside his community under *Gandharva Vivaha*, just in the presence of God and without any societal approval. However, marriage practices, beliefs and rules vary widely by region, caste and community. Marriage arrangements constitute a key site for distinguishing groups from one another, preserving lineage, and in consolidating and maintaining rank. Endogamous marriages are to be arranged by elders of the family to maintain purity of caste and preserve social status. What we find is that researchers have not gone too deep thereby getting a better picture of some of the dynamics and implications of such marriages especially in the Indian context.

The Special Marriage Act (1954) was a very important Act which allowed a man and woman belonging to different religions, castes or denominations to get married and retain their own religion even after marriage. This legal provision was a great step forward in support of inter-caste and inter-religion marriages in India. However, practices are in stark contradiction to what is legally prescribed and enshrined in the Constitution of India. Within the cultural diversity, the society does not practise arranged marriages only but also child marriages, endogamous marriages, that is marriage within the caste and sub-caste. Even today, in spite of legal provision for inter-caste and inter-religion marriages, such marriages are still not socially approved. An ideal marriage even today is considered to be one that is arranged by parents within the caste, and within the religious community. Inter-caste and inter-religion marriages have no social acceptance. Such marriages, even today are considered to be unconventional marriages and generally do not have the support and approval of the parents, kin group, and the society at large. In the past, such couples were socially boycotted and had to move out of the community, small town or city wherever they resided and find a place for themselves outside the kinship, caste, neighbourhood and village boundaries. Incidentally, even in modern societies, when families are not officially recognised or accepted but become the talk of the town, the girl and boy are often looked at as undisciplined, uncultured or often characterless.

Since such marriages lacked the support of families and kin group, the couple was frequently ostracised by the society and found it very difficult to sustain itself without family. The families of such inter-religion marriage couples have had to suffer the trauma and stress that was caused because of the social boycott. The most severe punishment that could be meted out to a person was to be disowned by his family and the community. The punishment was much more severe in the case of inter-religion marriages than in inter-caste marriages. Again, the severity of punishment for such couples depended on the social distance between two castes. Hypergamy (when a lower caste woman married a higher caste man) was always a preferential form of marriage in Indian society. But hypogamy (when a high caste woman married a lower caste man) was never permitted in the Hindu caste system. In fact, in a number of cases of hypogamous unions the couples often met with severe punishment; they were publicly lynched. The young couple are killed by tying them with a rope to a tree and stoning to death by the people of the village. This is often referred to as 'honour killing'. Hindus and Muslims have always been seen as juxtaposed—having the maximum social distance between them. This can be explained in terms of the historicity of the relations between Hindus and Muslims, the partition of the country and the historical fact that a majority of Muslims in India are converts from lower castes—which have also resulted in a caste-like hierarchy within the Muslim community in India.

The study on inter-religion marriages in India is a result of lifelong experiences of people. It is a difficult area of study especially when it comes to Hindu-Muslim marriages and explores the implications, relationships, problems of getting married, the marriage itself, its impact on the families of the husband and wife in question, the impact of such marriages on children and experiences of the couple, their parents and their children. Roberts (2002: 5) states that biographical methods are of particular value in determining how life experience can be understood within contemporary and structural settings and has the important merit of ordering the task of understanding major social shifts, by including how new experiences are interpreted by individuals within families, small groups and institutions. They provide an opportunity for detailed investigation of people's personal perspectives for in-depth understating of the personal context within which the research phenomena are located and for very detailed subject coverage. They are also particularly well suited to research that requires an understating of deeply rooted or delicate phenomena or responses to compose systems, processes or experiences because of the focus and the opportunity they offer for classification, understanding and details.

This study is biographical in so far, as we tried to recreate the lives of the respondents through their case-histories, and autobiographical in nature because both the authors and the respondents had inter-religion marriages. The personal experiences of the authors have provided deep insights into the understanding of inter-religion marriages in India. Our interaction with most of the couples in such marriages has been more of sharing of experiences rather than one sided monologues. We have chosen only Hindu-Muslim and Sikh-Muslim marriages for this study because these are the most difficult of all inter-religion marriages in India considering the history of Hindu-Muslim or Sikh-Muslim marriage relations starting from the Mughal period, independence movement and subsequently Partition. All these factors, individually and collectively have left a very deep and long lasting impact on the minds of Hindus and Muslims and their relations in the post-independence era which have been marked by frequent communal riots and communal violence in different parts of India. Gujarat, Moradabad, Lucknow Maharashtra and Delhi have been a witness to many such expressions of communal hatred.

Henceforth in the expression of Hindu-Muslim, Hindu will also include Sikh, because Sikh-Muslim marriages are equally problematic and difficult in India as are Hindu-Muslim marriages, and, there were at least five cases of Sikh-Muslim marriages in our sample of fifty couples. Hindu-Muslim marriages are not only seen as a threat to the community but also seen as an expression of loss of honour for the community whose daughter gets married to a person of another religion. We have also heard and read of instances of killing of such couples who have entered into inter-religion marriages, especially Hindu-Muslim marriages, in the recent past which have been reported in the newspapers and electronic media.

The most difficult task was not only identifying couples in Hindu-Muslim marriages because many such couples denied that they had inter-religion marriages due to fear of social opposition or even fear of communal violence erupting as a result of their marriage. But, also, once identified it was very difficult to obtain the consent of the couple to be interviewed or to be a part of the study. The couples were very reluctant to talk about their experiences. They were too scared that if the study revealed their identity, they would get into trouble. In spite of all our assurances that the present study is highly confidential, we were able to persuade only a small number of people to respond or share their experiences of inter-religion marriages with us. Not only was it difficult to persuade couples of inter-religion marriages to participate in the study, it was even more difficult to get the consent of the couples to interview their parents because of the opposition they had faced at the time of their marriages and many parents had still not accepted such marriages. It was also felt that the women did not wish to subject their parent to re-living the experiences and the agony of their marriages once again.

Collecting data on a sensitive issue like inter-religion marriages and that too Hindu-Muslim marriages was a very challenging task. Most inter-religion marriages were a very quiet affair. There was minimal celebration and only a very intimate group of family members and friends were invited. Sometimes even they were not invited, in some cases only friends were invited especially when it is a registered marriage. The tasks of contacting such couples became even more difficult because many couples and their families denied that an inter-religion marriage had taken place in their family. It was only by word of mouth that one could get to know of inter-religion marriages in an area. Sometimes even the neighbours did not know that an inter-religion marriage had taken place especially in cases where conversions happen. This was particularly true of Muslim-dominated areas where the bride-groom was a Muslim and the bride was a Hindu.

In case of newly married couples, the family often denied that an inter-religion marriage had taken place. There was extreme silence about it so that people did not get to know about it. The effort on the part of the girl to be accepted into the family often intensified the process of acquiring symbols of the 'other' culture and some of the Hindu girls even started wearing a burqa to gain acceptance. This made it even more difficult for the researchers to identify inter-religion couples.

Very often the children of such marriages were also difficult to identify. Socialisation of the children by the senior members of the joint family and the parents was such that the children learnt to identify themselves in most cases with the family, culture and religion of their father. There was a deliberate and special effort to assimilate them into the culture and traditions of the father's family and this can well be explained because of the patrilineal structure of our society. The explanation given in most cases was that this early socialisation of the child spares him/her an "identity crisis" later in life. In many cases, the children of such couples who were interviewed (age group 5-10 years) were not even aware that their parents belonged to different religions. Some parents prevented the researcher from interviewing the children—the parents did not want the children to become aware of the fact that their parents belonged to different religions. This made the task of the researchers even more difficult. The facts stated above explain why the parents of the couples interviewed and the children of the couple in inter-religion marriages are disproportionately smaller than the number of couples interviewed.

Not all the parents living in Delhi and elsewhere were willing to be interviewed. It was even more difficult to contact the parents of the women who were willing to be interviewed. Some of the women in the sample dissuaded us from meeting their parents. They did not want to subject their parents to the trauma caused by their marriage once again. "I do not want my parents to relive the pain of my marriage once again. Please do not interview them. I will tell you what they had suffered but please spare my parents", were the comments of some of the women whose parents had not been able to reconcile themselves to the inter-religion marriage of their daughter.

Gender, more than community seemed to influence the degree of parental and family opposition. The parents of the men who had inter-religion marriages were more accessible for interviews and therefore the percentage of parents of the men in the sample far exceeds the number of parents of women in the sample. This sample also reveals an important fact that the pain and suffering of the parents of the women was more than that of the parents of the men which is well reflected in the sample and it has its own sociological explanation.

This study was planned as a three-generational study because marriage is a process which involves not just one generation but a minimum of three generations. The impact of a marriage is deepest on the parents, the couple and the children. Therefore we have concentrated on three generations. It is often said that marriage influences not only the three generations but has an impact on all future generations, because children born of a marriage carry the lineage forward and they have the responsibility to carry forward the customs, values and traditions of the family. In inter-religion marriages the task of the children becomes more difficult because the parents belong to two different religions, cultures, customs and traditions. And, if regional differences accompany all these differences, the diversities get further compounded and it may involve not only comprehending and adjusting to two different cultures and traditions, but also at times learning two different languages. How the children cope with this situation becomes an important part of the study because their adjustment to these two different cultures, tradition and religions influence their own marriages and the future of their children and of future generations.

A sample of fifty couples was selected through the snow ball sampling technique. They were teachers, administrative staff or their relations staying near the universities. It was felt that the universities provided a more liberal environment and were more conducive to inter-religion marriages. It was, therefore, by choice and also by chance that the sample was selected from the three universities of Delhi. However owing to sensitivity of the issue, most of the information was verbally transmitted. It is a three generational study and respondents were selected from Jamia Millia Islamia, Delhi University and Jawaharlal Nehru University. The research also focused on parents of both the spouses whenever possible and also their children.

It was, therefore, important to study how inter-religion marriages come about, in spite of these socio-political conditions, how these marriages affect the couples, their parents and their children. The study is an attempt to explore answers to following questions:

(i) How do such marriages take place in spite of strong social opposition and political pressure?
(ii) How does the couple cope with social opposition from the family and society at large?
(iii) What is the impact of inter-religion marriages on the parents, the couple, close relatives and children of such couples? In other words what is the impact of such marriages on the three generations in question?
(iv) To what extent do such inter-religion marriages contribute to the secular ethos of the society?
(v) What is the impact of such marriages on creating a secular ethos in the society?
(vi) What mechanisms need be evolved in support of such marriages, if we have to move ahead on the road to secularism?

It is a well known fact that marriages in India are not between individuals but between families. The impact of all marriages and inter-religion marriages in particular are felt not only by the couples and their parents, but by the entire families had a long lasting impact on the children as well. Therefore, it was felt that apart from the couples, parents of both women and men should be a part of the study as well as close relatives and friends of such couples were interviewed in as many cases as was possible. Children of such couples who were in the age group of 10 years and above were included in the study whenever they were available and if the parents gave us permission to interview the children. The study was not confined to Delhi alone because many parents and close relatives of the couples were not living in Delhi. We tried to contact and get in touch with as many parents and close relatives and friends of the couples living in and outside Delhi. In addition, respondents in Mumbai, Lucknow, Bangalore, Hyderabad, etc. were contacted and in cases where prior consent was obtained the parents and other close relatives were interviewed. Apart from the couples and their close relatives, intensive interviews were also conducted with Hindu/Sikh-Muslim intellectuals, religious leaders, youth of both religious communities to see their responses and reactions to inter-religion marriages in India. Interviews were also held with important heads of NGOs working for the empowerment of women, to see what role the NGOs can play to provide support to people who marry outside their religion as Indian society has still not reconciled itself to the idea of inter-religion marriages.

Inter-religion marriages are too far-fetched. In fact, even inter-caste and inter-regional marriages are not easily acceptable. On account of lack of support from the society, it becomes very difficult for such marriages, i.e. inter-religion marriages to survive without family and social support. The study, therefore, was seen as a challenge because even the researchers got only limited support from the couples and their families, close relatives and friends.

2

Marriage, Family and Religion in Modern Society

All over the world, the old social order is giving way to a new one. In the West it began with the Renaissance and the Reformation and since then the change is continuously unabated. The major events as chronicled by the eminent social historians are the Renaissance, Reformation, Enlightenment, emergence of Positivism and the consequent scientific age. Between these events and later three great revolutions: French, Industrial and the Soviet followed by one another have shaken the world. These catastrophic events in their wake released a variety of forces for social change that could be described as truly titanic. Broadly the factors are valuation, scientific, technological, social and economic which caused or led to these events. They are inter-related even though the degree of inter-relation is always open to empirical investigation. Nevertheless there does exist an unambiguous correlation between the scientific technological and social and economic dimensions of change. Individualism, equality and liberty, and secularism are crucial value-oriented changes which can be outlined in the modern times. The essence of individualism in the post-Renaissance modern view is that the individual is at the centre of the social world and he/she is unique and a supreme model entity, who has certain inalienable rights and basic duties which represent basic conditions for the realisation of his personality. Equality and liberty are sought after in economic, political and social and cultural spheres and have evident aspects of values, ideologies and belief systems. Secularism heralds rejection of the sacred dimension inputs, metamorphosis of thought and transformation of society, for it involved changes in both the modes of thinking and the basic activities of man and consequently in the social structure of society. The immediate result is the undermining of the religious basis of the major institution of marriage and family. One of the universal features of the pre-industrial societies all over the world was the system of arranged marriages. In such a circumscribed society the marriage contract is looked upon as an agreement between two families rather than between two young individuals. Love was not considered a necessary prelude for testing the relationship.

Marriage is one of the universal social institutions established to control and regulate the life of mankind. It is closely associated with the institution of family. In fact both the institutions are complementary to each other. It is an institution with different implications in different cultures. Its purposes, functions and forms may differ from society to society but it is present everywhere as an institution. In *History of Human Marriage,* Westermarck (1921) defines marriage as the more or less durable connection between male and female lasting beyond the mere act of propagation till after the birth of offspring. He further emphasis, marriage is a contract for the production and maintenance of children. Robert Lowie (1925) describes marriage as a relatively permanent bond between permissible mates and is the approved social pattern whereby two or more persons establish a family.

Marriage is considered as an important institution, essentially because it is the deepest and most complex involvement of human relationships and symbolically the cornerstone of society. It is a basic structural element and a part of the social system. With marriage, an individual is assigned a definite role in the family that once again brought into focus the joint family, kin group and religious practices. In India, particularly since caste and religion are basic criteria in the selection of a mate in the kin-oriented choice, self-choice and love-matches are looked upon with complete disapproval.

Marriage is regarded in all human societies as a sacrament, that is, as a sacred transaction establishing a relationship of the highest value to man and woman. In treating a vow or an agreement as a sacrament, society mobilises all its forces, legal as well as moral, to cement a stable union.

According to Hindu religious ethics, marriage was not merely a union of two bodies but that of two souls. K.M. Kapadia (1988) observes that it was a religious bond and means of fulfilling the *purushartha.* This particular concept was considered to be ordained by the Vedas, for it was believed that *dharma* was to be practised by a man together with his wife. The Hindu marriage is not really a social contract but a religious sacrament. It results in a more or less permanent relationship between a man and woman. Their aim is not merely physical pleasure but spiritual advancement. According to the Hindu scriptures, marriage is the foundation of all religion activities. In the words of Kapadia, 'marriage is primarily for the fulfilment of duties; the basic aim of marriage was dharma'.

Islam exhibits a similar model to Hinduism. Muslims observe endogamous rules pertaining to class, race, sect and religion.In the Muslim community, marriage is universal for it discourages celibacy. Muslims call their marriage *Nikah,* a contract made between two persons of the opposite sex with the object of intercourse, procreation and the legalising of children. The bridegroom makes a proposal to the bride just before the wedding ceremony in the presence of two witnesses, a *maulavi* or *Qazi* (a learned teacher of Islamic law). It is a matter of tradition among the Muslims to have marriage among equals. Marrying idolaters and slaves is also not approved. Marriage amongst Muslims is soluble, and divorce is granted under certain conditions. They are two types of divorce (Talaq) *Khula* where divorce is initiated at the instance of the wife and *Mubarat* where the initiative may come either from the wife or from the husband. *Talaq* represents one of the ways according to which a Muslim husband can give a divorce to his wife as per the Muslim law by repeating the dismissal formula thrice. The *talaq* may be affected either orally by making some pronouncements or in writing by presenting talaqnama. Divorce as recognised by the Shariah Act 1937 provides for three forms of divorce: *Illa, Zihar* and *Lian*. There is also provision of divorce as per the dissolution of the Muslim Marriage Act 1939.

The Sikh marriage is not merely a physical and legal contract but is a holy union between two souls where physically they appear as two individual bodies but in fact are united as one. The Sikh marriage ceremony is also known as *Anand Karaj* meaning 'blissful union'. The *Rehat Maryada* which is the official Sikh code of conduct specifies that no thought should be given to the perspective spouse's caste, race or lineage. As long as both the boy and girl profess the Sikh faith and no other faith they may be joined in wedlock by the Anand Karaj ceremony.

Anand Karaj consists of the couple revolving around Siri Guru Granth Sahib four times as the *Lavan* (marriage hymns) are being recited. The marriage ceremony is conducted in a gurdwara or at the bride's home or any other suitable place where the Guru Granth Sahib is duly installed. A priest or any Sikh (man or woman) may conduct the ceremony, and usually a respected and learned person is chosen. The Sikh marriage is monogamous. In the case of a broken marriage, divorce is not possible according to the Sikh religious tradition. The couple can, however, obtain a divorce under the civil law of the land. Marriage, in Sikhism, is regarded as a sacred bond in attaining worldly and spiritual joy.

Catholics consider marriage as *Sacramento Continuum*. It must be performed by the Catholic Church to be valid and marriage cannot be dissolved. Protestants believe in the sanctity of marriage but divorce is allowed among them. It was St. Augustine, back in the fifth century, who formulated the classic statement of the three "goods" of marriage as loyalty, children, and indissoluble unity. Marriage, it is said, 'was ordained for the procreation of children, to be brought up in the fear and nurture of the Lord, and to the praise of His Holy Name.'

In India Hindus, Muslims, Christians and Sikhs all tend to follow strict religious endogamy by arranging marriages. The functional significance of arranged marriages was two-fold. It prevented the possibility of any prior loyalty on the part of the husband for his wife and checks the development of special emphasis on the conjugal relationship. To summarise this part of our discussion, we have tried to analyse that all religious bodies, like all closely knit and integrated groups, are concerned with the behaviour of their members, especially in matters that affect their relations to their groups. Naturally, then they are opposed to the marriage of their members with persons of another religious faith. Chief amongst the reasons for this are the threat of such marriages to group membership, their interference with religious observances, their disorganising effect upon family life and child rearing.

The family forms the basic unit of social organisation and it is difficult to imagine how human society could function without it. The family has been seen as a universal social institution and inevitable part of human society. According to Burgess and Lock (1939) the family is a group of persons united by ties of marriage, blood or adoption constituting a single household interacting with each other in their respective social role of husband and wife, mother and father, brother and sister creating a common culture, characterized by common residence, economic cooperation and reproduction. It includes adults of both sexes at least two of whom maintain a socially approved sexual relationship and one or more children own or adopted of the sexually co-habiting adults.

Nimkoff (1947: 8) says that the family is a more or less durable association of husband and wife with or without children or of a man or woman alone with children. He further states that family is a group defined by sex relationships sufficiently precise and enduring to provide for the procreation and upbringing of children. Kingsley Davis (1941) describes the family as a group of persons whose relations to one another are based upon consanguinity and who are therefore kin to one another. Malinowski (1945) observed that the family is the institution within which the cultural traditions of a society is handed over to a newer generation. This indispensable function could not be filled unless the relations to parents and children were relations reciprocally of authority and respect.

In the midst of great social, economic, and political change, over the centuries, India has a long heritage of stable family life, and family structure. The spirit of family solidarity has remained a sustaining power which has provided meaning to the daily lives of the Indian people. The traditional pattern of living was that of a joint family, whose members were bound together, by ties of common ancestry and common property, and often common subsistence.

Family in India is still a very strong institution and one cannot think of life without the family. Even in extended families where children have physically moved out of the family, family ties continue to be very strong. Although the number of such families had decreased over the years and size of such families has become smaller, the joint family continues to be an important institution in rural as well as in urban India. Traditionally and even today to some extent marriages continue to be arranged by parents or the family and marriage is a bond between families and kin groups.

In India, the joint family system is the norm and marriages are largely arranged by parents and elders of the family. The spouses themselves may have very little control over whom they marry. Thus a certain social satisfaction is maintained. Parents have control over the family members as they are the ones who decide whom their children will marry. Besides, the chances to preserve and continue the ancestral line are enhanced, as parents will choose a partner of the same caste, creed and social background. The kinship group is strengthened as mates are selected from among the kin, and with the consultation of the family members, not necessarily with the concerned mate. The family property is also consolidated, and extended, as no inheritance goes outside the family, it is within kinship marriages. Thus the principle of endogamy is preserved.

Today, radical changes are taking place in the sphere of civic, social, economic, and cultural life, which are affecting the pattern of family living. Better educational facilities, increased wage earning opportunities, and improved social occupations have had an impact on the traditional family structure. The family which is the most conservative institution next to religion is also affected by the process of modernisation. M.S. Gore (1968) remarked that there is a shift from the 'sacred family' which is centred on moral and religious values, to the 'secular family', with its more rational and pragmatic philosophy, which encourages family members to adopt new goals for themselves and for the community. These encourage the people to develop individualistic attitudes which enhance the probability of making independent decisions on matters related to marriage practices. The family system is thus exhibiting a loosening of its firm grip on the traditional pattern of mate selection, and permitting a certain amount of freedom to the young. The freedom may be that they are permitted to see the partner before marriage, in the presence of a chaperon, and in some cases, may give or withhold their consent, which may not always be respected.

Although arranged marriages are still a way of life, modifications in these are observed in recent times in large urban areas and among the educated youth. Boys and girls are given the opportunity to participate in the decision-making process of mate selection. It is quite common to find advertisements in the newspapers, for suitable partners, as this is a useful and convenient way of reaching out to a large segment of the population. Many matrimonial websites for match making exist on the net. In these the parents/relatives upload the details of the boy/girl along with their photographs and invite suitable matches. This is a quick and convenient way of finding a suitable match as it has exposure to the larger section of the community than the advertisements in the newspapers.

Most of the youth are brought up to believe that their parents and close relatives will do their best to find the most suitable match for them. Hence, they are prepared to marry the partner chosen by the family. Also, boys and girls are not allowed to mix or meet. Hence, there would be no opportunity for them to find their own match. Any young person meeting another of the opposite sex, especially a girl meeting a boy is considered immoral, and may not find a match due to that.

A marriage of choice is frowned upon, and emphatically discouraged, and the pair is considered non-conforming. Yet young people, more recently, tend to select the person they want to marry, and ask their parents for approval of their choice. However, this is limited in urban areas. Such marriages, where the partners decide to marry without their parents having selected the mates do not get the approval of parents, and often the dowry is not given. As a consequence, the parents of the boy, do not easily accept the girl. The other reason for not accepting such marriages is the violation of the traditional role that is denied to the parents of the boy and the girl. If there has been a self selected match in a family, the younger siblings will be branded, and the family will find it very difficult to find matches for them.

The practice of religious endogamy among Indians is a very well known fact. Undoubtedly those who marry inter-religiously follow an unconventional pattern and are prepared to accept the consequences of such a marriage. Most religions either prohibit or discourage marriage between one of their devotees and someone of a different faith. William Goode (1959) observes that the religious pattern of those strictly brought up is usually so efficacious that they desire no one of an alien faith. Despite all these religious restrictions, we find. a few individuals have overcome the religiously prescribed norms of mate selection and married by self choice. There is no doubt that a number of factors narrow the range of conscious choice. This range includes factors and forces of a wide variety and yet basically they are not different from those involved in any other aspect of human behaviour and social phenomenon. A basic factor that plays a significant role in self choice in inter-religion marriages is love.

The Contemporary Conception of Marriage

The number, the nature, and the changing proportion of mixed marriages must also be considered against the background of some current conceptions of marriage. The first of these, and foremost in certain respects, has been the change in the conception of the nature and control of marriage. Not only was the marriage ceremony solely a religious rite, but the sacred norms dictated the conditions under which the marriage might occur and, in certain rare cases, be terminated. The Roman Catholic conception of marriage as a sacrament, still maintained, is an example of such a conception of marriage. Behind this shift has been the slowly declining influence of the church in the control of marriage per se. In the Western world, marriage is rapidly losing its religious character, and increasingly tends to become a secular arrangement. Even the solemnities of a church service have tended to become secularised, being often made the occasion for conspicuous consumption and much-valued publicity. What was at one time a religious service is often turned into a stage-managed performance. The forms are maintained, but they have been emptied virtually of all their original meaning, as is borne out by the fact that many couples without any religious affiliation whatever will go through all the motions of a church wedding because it is considered socially the thing to do. Increasing numbers of marriages, in this and the other sense, are celebrated outside the church. To those for whom science has become the secular religion of the day, Malinowski, far from urging the abandonment of the sacrament of marriage, on the contrary shows that the institution of marriage and the family can be endowed with new values which can render their stability and sacredness as great as they have ever been.

Supporting this change has been the increasing

secularisation of our Western life and thought, to which reference has been made earlier in this book. A secular society is one in which resistance to change is at a minimum. It is rational and open-minded to a point often of indifference to the old and the sacred. It is a society in which a wide choice of conduct is permitted to the individual, including marriage. Secularisation combines many elements like the spread of science, increasing material well-being, the diffusion of education, and the encouragement of the critical faculty. Similarly, its influences ramify into many directions. The rejection of older, traditional ideas about mate selection and marriage certainly is one of these. The reduced control by the church over the behaviour of its members, including their marriage, is another.

Individualism is a complementary value that is much emphasised as a basis for marriage in contemporary modern society. The purpose of marriage, according to this conception, is the happiness of the mates and their respective personality development. A good marriage is one that contributes fully and freely to the development and enrichment of the personality of its contractors. On the other hand, a poor marriage is one that hinders it. This individualistic trend expresses itself in freedom of choice of mate, often disregarding the advice and admonition of parents, kinsfolk, pastor, priest, rabbi, or any of the traditional values and modes in mate selection. One of the most distinctive current emphases regarding marriage is the high premium set upon romantic attraction. As presently interpreted, this means that you marry solely for love, that marriage is the final realisation of romantic attraction.

Marriage Ceremonies

In an inter-religion marriage, the nature of the marriage ceremony acquires special significance, in view of the different religious backgrounds of the husband and wife. Respondents, who had consented to the repetitive forms of marriage, had done so to win the approval of their parents. In some cases when the couple decided to live in, the parental wish was to sanctify the union with a religious ceremony. Interestingly, many couples had a combination of more than one type of marriage ceremony. For example, some had a registered marriage followed by a *Nikah* (Muslim marriage), others had both the Hindu marriage ceremony, i.e. *Arya Samaj* and also the *Nikah*. Most of those who were converted to Islam actually practised Islam after marriage. Some only converted at the time of marriage and started practising it after marriage.

Some couples had combination of all types of marriage ceremonies: registered marriage, Arya Samaj and also *Nikah*. This was sometimes instrumental in winning the support of both the families. In few cases, although conversion had taken place before the *Nikah*, women never practised Islam and their husbands also did not enforce it on them. In one case a couple living in an independent house. The wife is a strict vegetarian and the husband is a non-vegetarian which she may not have been able to practise if she had lived in a joint family. The parents of the boy have still not accepted their marriage.

In cases where the parents of the girl and the boy agreed to the marriage, the couple tried to please them by having Hindu marriage rituals as well as *Nikah*. In cases where the parents of the girl and the boy both disapproved of the marriage, the couple tried to win them over by converting the girl but if the couple was highly educated, the chances were that they would opt for a registered marriage. Marriage ceremonies, therefore, reveal a lot: the socio-economic background of the couple and their families and also the attitude of the parents to their marriage as also the social environment within which the marriage takes place.

The Indian family has been subjected to stress and strain and in spite of resistance to change over centuries, is slowly undergoing a process of some significant change. The institution of the family is still the core of Indian society, and has not experienced a general disintegration. An important factor in Indian families is that when two individuals marry, there is a union of the families of the two spouses. The two families hence are usually compatible in creed, race, caste, region and class.

Patterns of Mate Selection

Love has played a decisive role in mate selection, yet the romantic ideal mate is not a sudden discovery but has its roots in the pattern of socialisation. According to Bambwale (1981) age is not the absolute criterion for the choice of a mate but plays a pivotal role. Educated women show a preference for men better educated than them. Common interests as well as academic background have played a vital role in mate selection. At the same time, character which has its roots in the traditional Indian religious ethics has played a dominant part in the choice of a life partner.

Other factors such as physical beauty, intelligence of the partner, compatibility have tilted the balance in favour of the partner in the final selection. Thus, there are many factors which contribute in choosing a partner. At the turn of the century, the concept of love had not attained the level of a mass phenomenon in Western society. It was confined to the feudal royalties and other feudal aristocratic strata. The aristocrats were more actively interested in winning love from their ladies. In those days love was not viewed as a 'boy meets girls' phenomenon. It was expressive of masculine valour, ardour, adventure, and most importantly, chivalry. It gained wider social implications only when the ideology of individualism became a dominant force and further, when industrialisation and urbanisation began to make their headway. At a later stage, the mass media of communications assumed immense proportions and today they are obviously the most powerful agencies in the diffusion of the creed of romantic love.

In American sociological literature one comes across various characteristic strands of thought on the theme of love. According to Zick Rubin (1968), love can become the greatest element in a decision or action relating to choice. Rubin further thinks that romantic love can be measured and assessed to find out if the involvement is deep or shallow. Landis and Landis (1963) take the same view and emphasise that the novelty of extreme differences in background or personality make up of individuals is sometimes believed to be conducive to romance. In Western culture moreover, the inextricable association between love and marriage gives it a unique status as a link between the individual and the structure of society. For these reasons these scholars feel that love is the deepest and the most meaningful sentiment. Another facet of love is that it is chiefly limited to premarital rather than marital relations. It is a phenomenon connected with courting in the strict sense of the term; William Goode (1959: 42) observes when 'two people become attached to each other by virtue of purely personal qualities, all other considerations being thrown to the winds.'

Goode further analysed this sociological phenomenon. He views love in a broad perspective focusing on the structural effect pattern by which societies keep in check the potentially disruptive effect of a love relationship on mate choice and stratification system. He makes it abundantly clear that if the factors of wealth, occupation, caste, age or religion do not substitute for love, they nevertheless constitute the social framework within when it operates. He also feels that the importance of love has been exaggerated in popular literature. Frequently it is believed to be a poor basis for marriages. People fail to take into account the selection process carefully, particularly the similarity of background of the couple. In this connection the situation in the West is different and in some ways special. The family unit is relatively independent of the larger kin group. Secondly, by falling in love the young person frees himself from the parental bond in order to enter the independent status of a spouse. From this angle, love may be viewed as a mechanism for filling the gap left by the decline of arranged marriages.

Another noted American author Ira Reiss (1972: 86), makes a socio-psychological approach on the theory of love. According to Reiss, the steps that proceed towards a love relationship after meeting are (i) awareness of one another or feeling of rapport (ii) self-revelation, followed by (iii) development of mutual dependencies or interdependent habit system, which finally leads to (iv) fulfilling personal needs.

Since these four processes turn one into the other and are constantly occurring, the above formulation concerning the development of love is called the 'wheel theory'. The wheel can turn in a negative direction and unwind, that is, the relationship can weaken when differences in opinion, taste, and competing interests clash.

Lopata (1973: 231) remarks that apart from all these characteristically American approaches to the sociological interpretation of romantic love, the most fundamental point to be noted is that with the present mood or mass romanticism the idea of love has been institutionalised and 'falling-in-love situations, popularity and personal characteristics have replaced older criteria for the selection of the mate'.

When we consider the situation in India, where a system of arranged marriage predominates, we observe that various social patterns exist to prevent romantic love from disturbing the traditional arrangements designed by the elders. Love is completely irrelevant in the traditional structure. In these societies the romantic behaviour is not conceived as a part of the ordinary process of mate selection and quite often those who fall in love have to brave storms of wrath.

Obviously there are some distinctive Indian variables, which have background significance in the life of the respondents and some of them are intertwining. Religious socialisation is an important aspect of the total process of socialisation in the life of an individual. Most individuals by the time they reach marriageable age have in varying degrees a religious or non-religious orientation. The significance of the parental opinions during the impressionable ages of the respondents can hardly be exaggerated. It will be generally observed that a favourable or tolerant attitude towards other religious groups adopted regarding formal social interaction is generally associated with the better prospects of marital success and happiness. Education is not only an asset to economic and social roles, as a step to employment, but also an asset in preparing for marriage as something valuable, changing the traditional conceptions of the roles and relationships of men and women. It has been accepted that educational institutions are obviously the first places where people come together in pursuit of common interests. It is generally believed that physical beauty is the most important factor for attraction. Accordingly, it is felt by Burgess and Locke (1953) that a person of the opposite sex possesses different degrees of sex appeal. Each individual's physical attraction is discriminating and selective. Beauty of face, grace of form, and allure of personal adornment separately or in combination are elements in physical attraction.

The majority of couples from this study were from coeducational colleges and universities. Consequently they became intimate during their college days. Associations in the colleges encourage free mixing and foster common interests have contributed to the ultimate choice. Besides these reasons, comparative data also show that individuals tend to select their mates who have an equal or almost an equal education.

The college campuses provide a perfect platform to the younger generation who would otherwise have been restricted from mixing freely. In India, the college life, is romanticised as a perfect phase where the freedom is not questioned. It also signifies a release from the tighter control of the society symbolised by the family. But higher education, apart from its environmental value has another aspect. Glick and Carter (1958) observed that higher educational attainment is correlated with greater marriage stability. Robert Blood (1963) corroborates with this view. He reasons that the couple has less of an difference with higher education and by the time Inter-marriage is opted for by the partners, they have gained maturity. The data certainly confirms this aspect to a significant measure. It shows that most of the women had married men either better-educated than themselves or at least equally well educated as themselves. There was only one interesting exception. Besides the level of education, the place of education is of equal importance in providing the necessary background for such unions. This is because away from home one has a better chance of mixing and meeting people of various groups.

A college or university campus setting could be a beginning to friendships that may ultimately lead to the lasting tie of marriage.

This factor is worth noting for, firstly while staying away from parents either for eductation and work with friends, hostels or paying guest accmodation, it is conceivable that the respondents lack continuous parental supervision. This is one of the crucial stages of socialisation of young individuals as they are somewhat away for a longer part of the year from the lifestyle lead by the parents. Secondly, this lack of parental supervision and guidance leaves an individual to make decisions on his/her own. As a considerable number of students attend coeducational institutions they have greater freedom to mix with the other sex. In fact quite often premature and thoughtless or impulsive friendships may also develop in this phase. Thirdly, college hostels and other places of residence other than that of the parents may have people of various religions staying together. This provides a greater chance to get acquainted with people from other religious groups and contributes to free inter-religious mixing.

Another salient social transformation taking place in the Indian family is the changing profile of Indian women, especially educated women are moving away from accepted family traditions and family controls, and are looking beyond their homes for self-expression. The spread of liberal education, the new ideas of equality and self-respect, the values attached to the development of individual personality, and the desire for economic and social independence, are some of the major factors which are affecting the pattern of marriage and family life, while drawing women away from their only field of responsibility, namely management of the home. The daughter in recent years is an economic asset and hence the age at marriage is gradually raised. Other factors such as occupational propinquity, self-choice of partner have entered the field of marriage and this has some bearing on the age factor. Along with the occupational factor there is a slow undermining of parental authority and the rising spirit of individualism, though these are rather slow social changes. To some extent, social and economic status acts as a decisive factor in mate selection. Women at work have a greater opportunity to meet men at work. A wage-earning woman has a certain confidence of financial independence which enables her to take independent decisions. Through friendship with various types of males, the notion of an ideal mate is crystallised and it may cut across religious differences. The principle of self-choice can be exercised and made feasible from a large group of acquaintances and friends which would normally be impossible in an arranged marriage.

It is observed that women who work invariably marry men nearest to their own profession. Sundal and McCormick (1951) found that among employed women there was a tendency to marry men who were employed in professions similar to their own. This was of greater consideration than consideration for financial gains. On the other hand, Hunt and Coller (1957) found that the choice in Inter-marriage was dependent not on similarities of profession of but on similarities of economic standards. Inter-personal factors of socio-psychological dimension play their part when a couple comes to know each other more intimately. Zick Rubin (1968: 758) mentions that when social lines are crossed it is men, who tend to marry down and it is women who tend to marry up. This has been termed by him as the 'mating gradient'.

Around 1950, American sociologists appear to have developed some formulations regarding the social and psychological forces which contribute to the phenomenon of inter-marriage. These formulations centre on the concept of homogamy. Burgess and Cottrell (1939), Burgess and Wallin (1943) find that mate selection is homogamous and advocate it. Burchinal (1963) called homogamy – endogamy or assertive mating, but Winch (1955) questioned it. Robert Winch challenged the principle of homogamy in mate selection and put forward the theory of complementary needs. Winch and his associates felt that the need of mate selection is based on the psychic make up of an individual engaged in mutual choice, and the basis of this choice is unconscious. Ktsanes (1955) reworked Winch's theory and found that the tendency to select a spouse unlike self in the total emotional make up far exceeds the tendency to select a spouse like self. Kerckhoff and Davis (1962) summarised that a significant contribution of complementarities in the mate selection process is assessed through value consensus.

Apart from these theories of mate selection, real choosing takes place for far more personal reasons. In romantic love the mate selection is also not free from a certain degree of determinism. Determinism as used here connotes that 'the social and the psychological experience of the past, markedly influence the way people respond and react in future' Lantz and Snyder (1969: 200). Such experiences stemming from either favourable or unfavourable relationships may result in patterning the mode of perception. If, as a result of previous experience one has learned to feel more comfortable with people, who enjoy literature and the arts, such an enjoyment becomes a value to him or her and he or she may tend to marry such a person. Thus the experience of the past can operate to move one towards or away from a given type of person. Likes and dislikes of certain qualities are nurtured in this manner. Most often there is little awareness of the impact of these past experiences on an individual.

Everyone tries to seek an 'ideal mate'. By an ideal mate it is meant 'that preconceived combination of emotional, physical and social characteristics that is embodied in one's personal image of the kind of person he or she would like to marry.' Lantz and Synder (1969: 210) One's preconceived notions about such characteristics as race, religion, nationality, education and socio-economic status often serve to eliminate a large number of people from one's marital choice. But these characteristics, although important, frequently operate without the person's awareness. Thus we find Klemer's (1970: 49) opinion that 'when you marry, you actually bring your entire past religious and cultural background with you and it remains with you' to be very true.

The Primary Challenges

Mostly inter-religion marriages are love marriages or self-arranged marriages and generally do not have the approval of the parents and the society as opposed to marriages arranged by parents within the caste and within the religious community. The degree of disapproval may vary from one case to the other and may be minimal in celebrity marriages. In such cases the celebrity status of one or both partners overrides religious differences of the partners. Even marriages within the caste which are not arranged by parents are usually not always supported by the parents. If the boy and girl belong to different religions that not only does not have the approval of the parents but is often accompanied by strong reaction from the families, relatives, friends and the two communities involved and if it happens to be a Hindu-Muslim marriage the reactions are even stronger. Hindus/Sikhs and Muslims are seen as antithetical to each other in terms of culture, traditions, religion and food habits. Politically they are seen as majority versus minority. Thus falling in love with a person of the 'opposite' religion or culture may be easy because opposites attract each other but the decision to get married is the most difficult one and getting the approval of the parents even more difficult.

Conversion by the bride or groom is the basic expectation of the family in case of inter-religious marriages. Generally it is expected that the bride should convert to the religion of the groom, although this may not always be the case. But when the groom converts to the religion of the bride, it is seen as a rare exception rather than the rule. The marriage in Hinduism/Sikhism and Islam is differently conceptualised. It is not only seen as a sacrament, but a religious bonding which spreads over seven births.

The process of social change has initiated a new emphasis on the family. Banot (1970) notes that increasing emphasis is now being placed on personal happiness and satisfaction of the couple. As we are moving towards individualism, the choice of a person is more important. The ideas of liberty and equality have changed the traditional understanding of the institution of family and marriage. However, these roles are changing as we face urban, industrial and technological advancements, by developments in science and education, which have opened up new opportunities and new roles for family members, and also due to the influence of Western culture. There has been a shift in importance from self-sacrifice on the part of the wife to satisfaction in marriage. The new emphasis on personal happiness in marriage has changed the mutual outlook of modern men and women towards marriage and family. The spouses prefer to choose each other themselves. Sometimes, young people of different religious beliefs, races, or classes, choose to be couples and so one speaks of mixed-marriages. Undoubtedly those who marry inter-religiously follow an unconventional pattern and are prepared to accept the consequences of such a marriage. There are strong attitudes about marriage within the religion, and marriages outside the religion are still not accepted by the society, especially in the rural and semi-urban set-up. Despite all these religious restrictions, we find a few individuals have overcome the religiously prescribed norms of mate selection and married by self choice.

3

Lived Experiences: Couples in Inter-Religion Marriages

Perhaps the best way to begin a discussion of inter-faith marriages is to do so concretely, that is, to tell in brief and simple fashion the stories of some people who have married outside their faith. This chapter presents some case histories of such marriages, selected from a collection of mixed marriages which we have gathered through the years. These particular cases are chosen because each shows some one outstanding feature or problem that recurs over and over again among our case histories. As mentioned in Chapter 1, a sample of 50 couples was selected for this study and detailed interviews were conducted in informal settings which can best be described as sharing of experiences. Since many of the couples were known to the authors, it was difficult to conceal the identity of the couples. However, sincere efforts have been made to conceal the identity of the informants and pseudonyms have been used to maintain confidentiality.

The detailed case studies of selected respondents are being presented below to show the life experiences of the couples in inter-religious marriages. The case studies are tilted in favour of the women in inter-religious marriages because the brunt of all the marriages and inter-religious marriages in particular has to be borne more by the women than the men. In all marriages, patrilineality is generally accompanied by patrilocality, i.e. women, after marriage, moves into the house—family of the husband—and she is the one who is expected to adjust to the family of her husband. So the case studies reveal the women's point of view more than the men's point of view. The woman is seen as the ego and all other relationships are seen from the perspective of the woman.

Case 1 : Ayesha

Ayesha was a Muslim, 76 years old, married to a Bengali Hindu, who was one year elder. He is a Bengali Hindu. Both were teachers in two different universities of Delihi. After retirement both have moved to Bangalore, where they were interviewed. They got married 60 years ago soon after partition in 1949. Ayesha shared her experiences of her inter-religious marriage, 'I was 16 years and my husband was 17 when we got married. Both were members of the Communist Party, I was imprisoned for one and a half year and sent to juvenile jail because I was not 18, at the time.'

Ayesha continued 'I belonged to a Khandan—a big extended family—which played an important role in the Freedom Struggle. I was in the first year of college when I met my husband. I started admiring him for his forceful speeches and his political ideology as well as his intellectual capabilities. I began visiting his house and found the family very warm, specially my father-in-law was a very nice, warm and a learned man. I had no mother-in-law'.

Ayesha described her parental family, 'I belonged to a family where women had very little access to education. My mother had five children; three daughters and two sons and she died at the age of 29. But she always discriminated against me and I resented it. I also resented the oppressive environment of the family where there were too many restrictions on women. After my mother's death, my grandmother brought us up. Since she was blind, it was a difficult task bringing us all up and especially because I was a rebel right from the beginning. My father was a great scholar and a sufi, greatly admired inside and outside the family.

Ayesha continued, 'I was the first girl in the family to go to college. I only had informal education at home and then privately appeared for high school examination from Aligarh. Later, I joined the undergraduate course in Anthropology in Lucknow University. I was in the first year of college when I got married. I completed all my education B.A., M.A., Ph.D., after my marriage. My husband and father-in-law always supported me'.

About her marriage, Ayesha said, 'It was a court marriage and I did not convert. I had only one child, a son, soon after marriage and he was brought up by my father-in-law and sister-in-law. My son came to live with me when he was nine years old. Before that, he lived with my father-in-law and sister-in-law. I brought him up like a Hindu and like a Bengali. I learnt Bengali from my father-in-law and other members of the family'.

With regard to reactions of close relatives to her marriage, Ayesha said 'my father was greatly criticised for my marriage and people in the family said his daughter had run away with a Hindu. But when my son was born, my father declared to all the members, holding my son's finger and announced to all the relatives that 'here is my daughter and grandson. I am going to maintain my relations with them. You can choose to meet me or not meet me, I don't care'. Everybody respected him all the more for his fearless stand and accepted me, with my husband and my son and respected us for our marriage'.

Ayesha also talked about her *Apa* (elder sister). 'My *Apa* also got married to a Hindu but converted him to Islam, renamed him Mohd. Usman and took him to our family. He was accepted but the children were always misfit in both the Hindu and Muslim communities—they were not fully accepted by either community. The daughter could never find a boy in the Muslim community who would marry her and found herself incapable of adjusting to a Hindu family. There were no marriage proposals worth considering even though she had a good job in the University but her frustration in life led to her deep depression resulting in her suicide. Her brother, *Apa*'s son is better adjusted to his life's circumstances and has married a Hindu but 'he is a slow achiever and suffers from a sense of inferiority', said Ayesha.

Ayesha's son did very well in life. He was an IAS officer and an IT expert, greatly admired by his colleagues, relatives and friends. Unfortunately, he recently died prematurely at the peak of his career. He was cremated at the electric crematorium. At home, *hawan* (*purificatory rites*, performed after the death of a Hindu) and *quran khwani* (reading of the quran after the death of a Muslim), both were performed after his death.

I have described two similar inter-religious marriages but both these marriages had a very different impact on the families and children. Ayesha brought her son up as a Hindu—who married a girl from a mixed marriage—a Punjabi mother and Bengali father. Apa on the other hand brought up her children as Muslim—both misfits in either community.

Ayesha's second sister, Fareeda, as a reaction to the marriage of her two older sisters, married a close relative; a Muslim. His only qualification was that he was a Muslim. It was an incompatible marriage. He died of cancer a few years after marriage. She had one daughter from the marriage. Fareeda's daughter was brought up by *Apa,* Ayesha's other sister mentioned above. Fareeda married a second time but again it was an incompatible marriage. The second husband also died leaving behind two children. The daughter by the first marriage hates her mother. Fareeda has settled in England. She is very attached to Ayesha and her family but is very critical of *Apa,* for she somehow holds Apa responsible for her daughter's hatred for her mother. But, perhaps it is the circumstances in which the daughter was trapped that explains the daughter's hatred for her mother.

Both Ayesha's brothers married Muslim women. All the Ayesha's brothers and sisters were very attached to Ayesha and her family. Initially, there was a lot of resentment and alienation but now all is well and Ayesha's house is always full of relatives from both sides, Ayesha's maternal kinsmen and her husband's close relatives. They were all a great support and strength to Ayesha and her husband specially when they were going through the crisis of coping with the death of their only child who died prematurely. Relatives from both sides, even those who have settled abroad, came to console Ayesha and her family.

Case 2 : Jasmeet

Jasmeet belongs to a Sikh family from Jammu. She lost her mother at an early age. She had two brothers and she was the only daughter. She did her Masters Degree in a Social Science subject. While she was a student, she fell in love with a Muslim boy who studied in the same class. She performed well in her examinations and registered herself for her M.Phil and later Ph.D in the same discipline. She got married soon after her M.Phil but did not disclose her marriage to anyone for about a year or two. She continued to live in the hostel without disclosing to anyone that she had got married. The marriage was a registered one but later *nikah* was also performed and she converted to Islam and as in the case of all such marriages she was given a Muslim name. Her husband belonged to a joint family of artisans settled in UP. He continued in his family business after the marriage. Jasmeet is 45 years old and has two sons aged 13 and 10.

Jasmeet's family never accepted this marriage. They, in fact, disowned her and, except for her younger brother who occasionally visited her, nobody ever tried to contact her. Unfortunately, the brother too died prematurely at a young age soon after his marriage. When she became pregnant with her first child, she contacted her father, thinking that the news of the expected grandson would melt his heart. But her father told her that if she wanted to return then she would have to leave her husband and abort the baby. When Jasmeet's father expired, nobody informed her. She came to know about his death after a year or so.

On the other hand, Jasmeet s in-laws accepted her totally, gave full respect and share of the property to her. Her in-laws often visited her and lived with her in her house in Delhi. Her husband's brothers, cousins and many other close relatives stayed with her family whenever they come to Delhi. Jasmeet's in-laws always showered a lot of gifts on her whenever she went to her husband's hometown on the occasion of *Eid* (Muslim festival) and *Bakr-e-eid* (Muslim festival of scarifice) in particular. Jasmeet adapted and adjusted herself to Muslim culture and lifestyle to such an extent that she observed *roza* (fasting) during the entire month of Ramzan and offered namaz and gave donations (*zakat*) during the holy month of Ramzan. Seeing her total adjustment, her husband also supported her and they both celebrated Holi and Diwali with their Hindu friends.

It is interesting that recently after her father's death, Jasmeet's brother and their wives repented and started meeting her, her husband and children. They even promised to give her share of the parental property.

After marriage Jasmeet and her husband tried to get accommodation in a mixed locality and were on the verge of shifting there when the residents of that area became aware of their inter-religion marriage, objected to their staying as they feared it could lead to a communal tension. So when they had no other option left, the couple had to move to a Muslim-dominated area of South Delhi.

Here Jasmeet is well accepted in the neighbourhood but even she had to work hard to win the love and affection of her in-laws, neighbours, friends and parental family. She is now well adjusted and feels that her sons will grow up in a very secular environment and decide whom they want to marry and their decisions will be supported by her and her husband irrespective of the religion, the girls belong to. But even such educated couples are apprehensive of the future of their children whenever there are cases of communal violence, political upheavals and cases like the Gujarat riots.

Children of inter-religion married couples are exposed to weird questions related to their religious identity. One particular incident happened to their elder son who was asked about his religious identity. The boy was asked who is his God—Allah, Nanak or Ram? Jasmeet is very happy and doing very well in her professional life, but still there is a sense of guilt and loss as all the ties were broken with her own maternal family and community. But on the other hand, what she has achieved is of significant value, she always cherished her upbringing as liberal, modern and progressive child. The broader outlook her parents had provided her during her childhood, has strengthened her immensely to meet the challenges of inter-religion marriage. She is happy to see some Punjabi traits emerging in her younger son, his fondness for Punjabi culture. She often jokes with her husband that 'you cannot do anything about genes, they are in the blood'. Living in a bicultural family is a experience in itself. It is so heart-warming to see different types of cuisine being prepared to meet the religio-cultural requirements of friends visiting them on *Eid*.

Case 3 : Mallika

Mallika was a Hindu woman aged about 64. She got married to a Muslim nearly 38 years ago. Both of them were teachers in the University. They liked each other and wanted to get married. But it was difficult as the woman was the only daughter of her parents and the man she wanted to marry was the only son of his parents. The man lost his father at an early age. He had four sisters, three of whom were married and the youngest was yet to be married.

There was considerable opposition from both sides but more so from the parents of the woman. Although the parents of the woman liked the man very much, they were apprehensive of all that their daughter might have to suffer because of the marriage. They were also apprehensive of the ability of their daughter to be able to adjust to a Muslim family. Also, both the families had suffered and experienced the partition and were witness to the hatred that existed between Hindus and Muslims during partition. They tried their best to dissuade the woman and the man from the marriage. But when all their efforts failed, they reconciled themselves to the marriage and participated in the marriage ceremonies. Mallika's brother and her close friend Ayesha (Case No. 1) were very supportive and played a crucial role in convincing her parents about the feasibility of the marriage. Both the marriage ceremonies were performed according to the system of Arya Samaj and the *nikah*. The parents of the woman participated in the ceremony of Arya Samaj and close relatives and friends of the man participated in the nikah ceremony.

The couple have two children, a son and a daughter with secular names. They could easily be Hindu or Muslim names. The couple lived for about 14 years in the Jama Masjid area in the joint family but after their children grew up and were school going, they moved out of the neighbourhood. Both the families gradually accepted their marriage. Their daughter got married to a Muslim and the son got married to a Hindu. Thus completing the cycle of Hindu-Muslim marriages in the family which confirms our hypothesis that inter-religion marriages contribute to the secular ethos of the society.

The Muslim family into which Mallika's daughter was married was part of the kin group of the husband. The proposal came from the boy's family and the marriage was celebrated according to Islamic rites, i.e. the nikah. There was no opposition from either side. In the case of Mallika's son's marriage, there was no opposition from the boy's parents but the girl's parents were strongly opposed to the marriage. The marriage took place without the consent or participation of the girl's parents. However, soon after the marriage, the girl's sister and her brother-in-law accepted the marriage and started interacting with the girl and her in-laws. The girl's younger brother has also resumed ties with the sister. But the parents of the girl have still not accepted their daughter's marriage. Perhaps this is so because they belonged to a small community of Brahmins of Uttrarakhand and being a very close knit kin group, they found it difficult to face their relatives. In fact, they have not even disclosed to their relatives that their daughter had married a Muslim boy. Although they know that the boy belongs to a very secular family which believes more in humanism as a religion rather than any particular fundamental ideology, the fact that the father of the boy is a Muslim, was the only sore point because of which they opposed the marriage.

The family under discussion is treated as an ideal Hindu-Muslim family. They celebrate both Hindu-Muslim festivals with equal fervour. Even such a family had problems when it came to the woman's job. Though she was highly qualified, when she first applied for a job in the University and got selected, she was told by the college authorities that had they come to know about her inter-religion marriage, she would not have been selected.

Case 4 : Fatima

Fatima was a Muslim woman aged about 57 years who got married to a Hindu of high caste—a Brahmin, about 35 years ago. She belonged to an orthodox Muslim family which did not accept her marriage to a Hindu. Initially, she was also very reluctant to marry a Hindu. She tried very hard to find a suitable Muslim boy failing which she agreed to marry a Hindu with whom she was working in an NGO. She is a teacher in the University and her husband works for an NGO. They have only one son who is now about 28 years. Initially, there was a lot of opposition and hostility from the woman's family but gradually they accepted the marriage over a period of time. However, the man's family never created any problem for the woman. They accepted her wholeheartedly. The couple had a registered marriage and the woman continues to practise her religion and the man continues to practise his religion. They are also considered to be as an ideal inter-religion couple. As far as the religion of the son is concerned, initially he was brought up by his maternal grandmother and he imbibed the religious values of Islam. But at the age of 10 or so, he joined his parents in Delhi and now has picked up the religious values from both his parents. The name of the son is also a secular name which could be taken as a Hindu or a Muslim name. The son said that initially, when he was young he was very confused about his religious identity because people asked him embarrassing questions about his family background. He enjoys the dual cultures of the two families—father's and mother's families, which he could never have experienced so intimately but for the different religious background of his parents. He said, 'now I am proud of my parents'. In spite of her marriage to a Hindu, the woman has been promoted to the position of a Professor in the University and her marriage has not come in the way of her professional career in the University.

Case 5 : Kanchan

Kanchan was a Hindu, aged about 65 years, who got married to a Muslim about 40 years ago. She belonged to a wealthy and educated family. The couple started meeting each other when they were both research scholars in the University. They decided to get married after a long courtship. The woman was unsure of the future of the marriage but after the long insistence and persuasion of the man, they finally got married. But the differences started brewing soon after the marriage. It was a case of incompatibility. There was a lot of opposition from the woman's parental family and also from the man's family. It was a registered marriage and soon after the marriage the couple went abroad. They stayed abroad for 3-4 years and had two sons. As time passed, the differences between the couple grew and they decided to live apart after about 20 years of marriage.

Kanchan never married again and raised her two sons in very difficult circumstances. The sons hardly met their father after their divorce. The father, however, got married about 10 years after the divorce. He got married to a Muslim woman who is much less qualified than his first wife and her socio-economic background is no match to the socio-economic status of the first wife. The first marriage ended in a divorce and the bitterness of the divorce has increased after her husband got married second time. The sons neither want to meet their father nor to do they want to even discuss their relationship with their father. The mother is looking for brides for her sons and she insists that both the sons want to marry Hindu girls. Unfortunately, however, so far she has not been able to find suitable brides for her sons.

Again the question arises, is it because of an inter-religion marriage and loss of identity for the boys that they are not able to find suitable brides for themselves? Or, is it that, after the divorce, Kanchan returned to her original religion, she dropped her husband's name from her own name and took on her maiden name? She also changed her sons' names from Muslim to Hindu names. This seems to have resulted not only in a loss of identity for the sons but in this case the shift and change in the identity of the mother which is reflected in the change in their names, has added to the complexities and problems in their lives and seems to be coming in the way of the marriages of the sons. As is clear in the above case that it is not the difference in religions which was the cause of divorce in Kanchan's case but incompatibility between husband and wife that seems to have resulted in the divorce. The aftermath of the divorce and reversal to the mother's religion has further exacerbated the problems of the mother and the sons.

Case 6 : Anjana

Anjana is about 76 years old. She is a Hindu and got married to a Muslim about 45 years ago. Both she and her late husband were highly qualified and were Professors from the University of Delhi. They worked together in the University for many years and then both went abroad where the husband did his Ph.D. They got married when they were studying abroad. They have one son who is about 40 years old and is still unmarried. Anjana belonged to an affluent and educated family and there was hardly any opposition from her parental family or from her husband's family against their marriage. They had their own independent house close to the University and as reported by her it was a very happy married life. It was almost a "problem free" marriage as she described it. Their marriage was a registered marriage and both of them had the freedom to practise their own religion. But, being a secular couple they hardly ever went to the mosque or the temple. However, they did perform the ceremonial part of their religions at home. They celebrates the Hindu as well as Muslim festivals; i.e. Holi, Diwali, Eid and Bakr-Eid.

Anjana and her husband were greatly respected by their colleagues in the University and had a large circle of friends within and outside the University. Their families were also very supportive and this was one of the reasons that made their marriage successful. However, the husband died prematurely about 15 years ago and now the wife and her son live together. The son is a well established journalist. But in spite of not having any problems in the marriage, the son who has a Muslim name has not been able to find a life partner of his choice and therefore continues to remain single. Is it by choice or is it because of the inter-religion marriage that he has not been able to get married, is very difficult to say. The son, when questioned about his marriage, often said 'what is the need to get married? I would rather not talk about it.' This does not seem to be a normal reaction. And, it reflects a pessimistic approach to life. Is this a result of inter-religion marriage which has led to a sense of insecurity or a loss of identity or is it a reaction to some other circumstances that have led to this pessimism is difficult to say?

Case 7 : Gurpreet

Gurpreet is a Sikh married to a Muslim. She is about 68 and her husband is also of the same age. They got married around 40 years ago. Both of them were teachers in the University. They have now retired. Both belonged to moneyed families but the families were not very well educated. The parents of the woman were strongly opposed to the marriage and disowned her completely after the marriage. It was a registered marriage. The husband and wife taught in the same college. They faced a lot of opposition by the administration in the college after their marriage and the husband lost his job when the Principal of the college came to know of their inter-religion marriage.

The case went to the court and the husband won the case. It became a political issue and the university teachers supported both of them. The husband was later employed in another college in the same university and his wife too got a job in the same college.

The couple have two sons, both have Hindu names and are very bright. They have done very well in life. We could not find out about the marriages of their sons. This couple fought against all odds, was well adjusted to each other and the society without their family support. The support of the friends and the university helped them to establish themselves and assert their identity. Although they had the freedom to practise their own religion, their communist ideology and practice was the only thing that they were proud of rather than their different religious backgrounds. They both felt strongly that such inter-religion marriages would truly contribute to the secular ethos of Indian society and children should be encouraged to opt for inter-religion marriages, learn to respect the religious values and differences of others. This would give India a true secular image and help in the growth and development of a secular society.

Case 8 : Farzana

Farzana was a Muslim woman, aged 68 years. She got married to a Hindu, ten years younger than her, about 35 years ago. The husband was a Hindu Brahmin from Kerala. The woman was quite a staunch Muslim working in the university as an administrative staff where she met her husband who was also an employee of the same university. She never wanted to marry a Hindu or anyone other than a Muslim. She tried her best to find a Muslim of her choice whom she could marry but when her efforts failed, she agreed to marry a Hindu gentleman who was her colleague. They were both in the administration. The marriage was a registered marriage. She continued to practise Islam and her husband also continued to practise Hindu religion after their marriage. Initially there was considerable opposition from both the families against the marriage but gradually it all subsided and she was accepted by her in-laws. But her own parental family which was not very well educated, and belonged to a small town in UP did not accept the marriage till the end. The couple had only son who felt totally insecure because his mother's family never accepted him. The family of the father which was settled in Kerala, hardly interacted with him and his mother because they were not able to visit the husband's parents very frequently in Kerala. The boy suffered a great sense of insecurity and loss of identity because he had no support from the family of either parents. The husband unfortunately died at a young age leaving behind his wife and son. This sense of insecurity was then extended to the wife as well and to give more security to the son, the woman encouraged the son to accept Islam which she thought was the best way to help the son to come out of the crisis. The son is around 30 years old and he is doing well professionally but has not been able to get married because Muslims refuse to give a girl to him in marriage and Hindus in any case would not accept him as their son-in-law. This is a clear case of loss of identity which got aggravated firstly because of an inter-religion marriage and secondly his father's death at an early age.

Case 9 : Razia Pathak

Razia Pathak is a Muslim Pathan woman aged 70 years. She was married to a Hindu Brahmin from Patna before marriage known as Neeraj Pathak. He converted to Islam before marriage as this was the pre-condition imposed by Razia. After marriage he became Rehmat Pathak. They got married when she was doing graduation at Lady Shri Ram College of Delhi University. Her husband practised all the rituals of his new religion. He offers *namaz* and fasts in the month of Ramzan. He cannot read the Quran in Arabic but he remembers a few verses.

Rehmat ate beef and non-vegetarian food before marriage. Therefore, they have not faced any problem on food issues or in general on other issues of everyday life. 'Conversion is necessary for me, for others it may not be important. Every marriage is taxing. In such a type of marriage adjustment plays a very important role. My husband never feels regression and suffocation. My husband told our children that his death ritual would be performed according to Islamic rituals. Property has been distributed and we got property from both sides', said Razia. There is no change in her lifestyle.

Both had successful careers and have retired. They have two married daughters. One of their daughters got married to a Hindu. 'It was a civil marriage and he did not convert as it was not important for my daughter', Razia confessed, 'but for me conversion was important because I am religious person. I have taught my children Islamic norms and regulations. Now they have to decide what they want to follow. They never forced them to follow any particular religion. I taught both my daughters the Islamic faith but they do not practise it regularly. I offer *namaz* but they don't'. When the children were small she persuaded them to offer *namaz* regularly but now she can only hope that they still practise what she has taught them. Their elder daughter is married in a Muslim family but the younger married into a Hindu family. Razia wanted her to marry a Muslim but it did not happen. 'At that time I was upset but now I am happy. In my opinion there is no hard and fast rule. It depends on both individuals, as in every marriage there has to be adjustment.' She said, 'I think that a person should marry within religion as it is easier for the couple to adjust. It would be hard to accept a person of a different religion but because my husband converted before our marriage so it is easy for me. If he had not converted then I would not have married him.'

Razia is a dominating partner. Her husband could not be contacted for interview, may be he was not willing. However, it was observed that after marriage, they stayed in Razia's parental house. Her family is quite influential politically. Both her daughters had love marriages.

Case 10 : Ambika

Ambika is a Punjabi Hindu woman married to Amir Zaidi. They are in their late sixties. Both of them studied at Aligarh

Muslim University and got married 35 years ago and are now settled in Delhi. Ambika has not converted. Nobody approved their marriage at that time. It took nearly six months for their parents to approve their marriage. They have two daughters and now their elder daughter has settled in the USA. At the time of this interview both their daughters were unmarried. They have been give the freedom to choose their partners themselves. 'The couple wanted their children to marry a person who is broad-minded. According to them, marriage is an adjustment. If there is a lack of understanding between the partners then the problem occurs. This does not happen due to belonging to a different religion. It is because of not understanding each other and it can happen in the marriage within the same religion or a different religion.

Both Amibka and her husband do not practise any rituals as they are cosmopolitan in their approach. Being a secular couple, they celebrate all festivals. Even Ambika's mother and in-laws both participate in each other's festivals. They have a Christian maid, so they celebrate Christmas along with *majlis* (religious gathering of Muslim on special occasions) and *havan*. It was interesting to note that their younger daughter Sanya who is 29 years of age practises Islam. She offers *namaz*, reads Quran and observes fasts. She did Bio-Chemical Engineering from Delhi University and her Masters from London University. She is a Health Consultant.

Amir is not practising Muslim, he is Muslim only in name. Religion was never an issue with both Ambika and Amir. They have no knowledge how their daughter got influenced by Islam. Sanya has not got married because she is waiting for the right person. She wants to marry a Muslim. She can marry a Hindu boy but it is her opinion that she will not be able to make the necessary adjustments. She is a very religious person and has studied almost all religions. She is secular and in their home every festival is celebrated and she respects all religions. She said, 'I studied almost all religions. But what I feel in Islam, I have not found in any other religion. I feel comfort and peace in this religion. I did meditation but I could not relax but when

I offer *namaz* I feel comfortable. I think that Islam is an ideal religion. I have accepted this religion on my own. I cover my head with a scarf and it was also my own decision.'

Sanya was sad that in their maternal grandparents' home they do not get appreciation and affection, because her maternal grandparents' family felt that the children are Muslim as they practise all rituals which are not acceptable. In her paternal grandparents' home the children are accepted and loved.

Being an offspring of mixed marriage, she has not faced any identity crisis. This is because 'In my case there is no confusion about my religious status. When people ask me about my religion I tell them that I am a Muslim so I have not faced any identity crises. But I think that parents should follow one religion for the sake of children. They should not confuse their children. If the mother does not follow Islam, it causes confusion for the children. There are differences between my mother and me about religion and there is no affinity between us. She is my mother so I can't fight with her. I respect her so most of the time I keep quiet.'

Sanya has a different perception of religion. Her parents are very liberal and this secular outlook they provided to their daughters might have been the reason for Sanya to explore other religious ideologies and philosophies and to adopt the ideology which convinced her heart and mind. This kind of socialisation and nurturing promotes pluralism.

Case 11 : Kamljeet Kaur

Kamljeet is a Sikh woman, married to Mohd Zahid, a Muslim. Both of them worked together in a media house. She was a journalist and they decided to get married very quickly. It took only two months. They lived together before they married to test their relationship since both of them were previously divorced. This was their second marriage. Kamaljeet's son from her first marriage and her brother-in-law stayed with them together as a family. In 1998 they got married in the court and her friend and her husband's brother and sister were present.

Their parents could not attend the marriage as Zahid's mother was not happy, This is because Zahid's ex-wife's brother got married to his sister. There was the apprehension in Zahid's family especially for his mother, that if he left his ex-wife then her brother-in-law might leave his sister. So there was pressure on him. That is the reason why her mother-in-law had problems accepting her. But she did not try to prevent them from marrying. Her parents were too old and were settled in Rajasthan.

Kamljeet's parents did not prevent her from marrying as she had a failed marriage previously and now they wanted her to be happy. They love her daughter Mahak from this marriage. Her brothers were against this marriage. No conversion took place in their marriage. Zahid said that 'conversion is not important .There is no need to enter into inter-religious marriage, if you want to convert a person. It is better to marry in the same religion. I am not a religious person. I don't practise any rituals. But I can't change my religion.'

Zahid is comfortable with Kamaljeet following her rituals and rites but he told her that only one thing he wanted to do was that her death rituals would be as per Islamic rites. This is because he loves her so much that he can't see her body getting burnt. This is the reason he wants to bury her after her death. Her in-laws tried to persuade her to convert but she has not converted. She is not sure whether she will convert or not.

After marriage their food habits have not changed. Kamaljeet does not eat beef. In Zahid's family, nobody eats beef for health reasons. Kamaljeet has no problems regarding her food habits. Zahid only brings *halal* meat (permissable as per Islamic law) to his house, his in-laws do not object to it. They even come and stay with them; while they stay with them they follow their daily *puja* (religious ritual performed by hindu) without any hindrance or hesitation. Their comfort level is very high with their son-in-law.

Kamaljeet doesn't feel apprehensive because of this marriage. This is because when they got married, they were mature. They took this step when they were confident. Zahid willingly accepted Kamaljeet's son from a previous marriage, who is 22 years old. He calls Zahid uncle and he follows Sikhism. When she got married, her son was mature enough to understand and he shares a very good relationship with his half-sister Diya, daughter from this marriage. They are like siblings. They fight and love each other even though there is a big age difference between them. They are close to each other. The reason for this is that her son was the only child and he looked forward to have another brother or sister and when she was born, he was happier than them.

According to Kamaljeet, her marriage is not taxing. They are a secular couple. In their home, her son follows Sikhism and her daughter follows Islam, as her father in Muslim, Kawaljeet has no problem. She celebrates all festivals, but without any rituals because they don't believe in rituals. They enjoy every festival. She teaches her children to respect all religions and to be a good human being and never fight because of religion.

She is determined that she will not force her children to marry in her religion or her husband's religion. She has chosen her partner herself. Therefore the children would have the right to choose their partners themselves.

For Kawaljeet, her first marriage was in the same religion and it was an arranged marriage. But it was not successful. This is because they were two different people. They were not compatible to each other. So eventually she decided that she could not continue resulting in breaking up the marriage. Now this marriage has taken place after many years. They fight but not so seriously that they would separate. They are living happily.

She doesn't want to recommend anything. She is a liberal person. People have the freedom to choose their partner, and if anybody wants to marry in the same religion it is commendable. But if they want to opt for inter-religion marriage they should have the freedom. But they should not marry inter-religiously for the sake of conversion.

Every inter-religion marriage is unique in terms of

experience. In fact this family is truly modern, woven into the pluralistic tradition. Each member of the family has independent space and respects each other's quest for freedom.

Case 12 : Surjana

Surjana is 45 years old. She is a south Indian Hindu Brahmin, married to Farhatulla Beig from Andhra Pradesh. They have known each other since childhood. They started liking each other and decided to get married. They got married in 1998. It was a civil marriage, i.e. court marriage. The parents of Farhatulla approved the marriage but his in-laws did not approve their marriage immediately. Their friends participated in their marriage.

According to Surjana, she didn't compromise on anything and nothing has changed in her life. Nobody converted in this marriage. They both practise their own religion. She was a vegetarian before marriage and remained one after marriage also. Non-vegetarian food is only prepared in their home when her in-laws are there. When her parents come they switch over to pure vegetarian food. Her husband has no problem, but children find it difficult to constantly alter their food habits. They have two children, a son and daughter aged 13 and eight years. Both husband and wife follow their own religion, both of them expose their children to their culture.

Children are asked to behave in different ways with both grandparents. Surjana's parents want to follow Brahmanical traditions. They are supposed to greet relatives in a traditional way. Similarly, Farahat's parents want their children to follow the Islamic way of life, since the father is Muslim. Though both Surjana and Farhat are a devoted couple and both of them are attached to their parents, they became distressed by the situation. Finally they agreed to give their children religious education in both the cultures. Since both the families are particular about their religious traditions, they keep shifting back and forth at times and this becomes an issue with children. This might have worked out as a satisfactory solution, but children have a way of growing, of noticing, and of talking.

At first, Surjana and Farhat would interpret the slips which the children made in conversation, but this created a very tense situation for them would only mean a temporary avoidance of the issue. As time went on, the children became increasingly puzzled. There were major differences like the way of life in both the cultures. Dual set of norms, patterns and preferences for food, dealing with attitudes of grandparents, as well as the attitude of their parents was becoming a task in itself. On Navrataras, there was no non-vegetarian food, no "unseemly" amusement, and no parties during Ramzan, sober observance of the day. Celebration of birthdays, cutting of cake and partying was not allowed by paternal grandparents, whereas maternal cousins had grand parties. They were leading a double life, as it were, a dual set of standards, two sets of teachings in an area which was emphasised as of the greatest importance in life. These were the continuing experiences, certainly of the children, and also of the couple. Fifteen years after their marriage, two young parents and two very attractive children were living in a state of confusion, tension, and uncertainty. Under other circumstances, this might have been a very happy family. As things stand, their future as a family is uncertain.

The complexity has increased because Surjana is a CEO with a reputed multinational company and Farhat is also a freelance media professional. Both of them are very busy owing to their professionl commitments giving the grandparents an opportunity to interefare in their life.

Farhatulla says that every marriage is taxing because a couple has to compromise, sacrifice and adjust then a marriage becomes successful. He doesn't want to comment on the marriages of others because making marriage a success depends on the individuals themselves. According to Farhat, they are secular and they celebrate the festivals of both religions. They are initiating their children into the teachings and practices of both religions, Islam and Hinduism. They offer namaz with him and also go to temples with their mother. He doesn't force her to follow a particular religion. Any marriage may succeed or not, it does not depend on inter-religion or inter-faith marriages. It depends on many other things. It may be education and how much one is able to adapt and understand each other. These factors are more important than religion. Surjana doesn't recommend anything. This is because she thinks that marriage is something which an individual has to decide on his own. The factor of religion may not be that important. According to her, if one wants to go in for inter-religion marriage then one should go for it. According to him, marriage is a gamble and in every marriage a couple has to adjust. For him, there is no comparison between both types of marriage.

These cases present so many facets of marriages between persons of different religious faiths. They are intended to reveal with the concreteness of reality what may happen in such marriages. Are these cases typical of what happens when people of different faiths marry? What is the real nature and difficulty in all mixed marriages? What is the outcome of such marriages? Do they lead to happiness or unhappiness? What do they mean for the children? How many such marriages are there? Is their relative number increasing or decreasing? Why do all religions oppose such marriages? Why is the opposition to such marriages becoming more and more pronounced? If you have made such a marriage, is the situation hopeless? Have some marriages of this kind been successful? And, if so, why? What constructive steps may be taken? These and other questions will be considered and answered in the succeeding pages of this book.

Thus so far, the more general aspects of inter-faith marriages have been pointed out. The differences between religious groups are fundamental and pervasive. They include differences in religious convictions and these are not unimportant. But they include much more. Behind the beliefs are differences in behaviour, in observances in daily life, in attitudes, in values, and in moral judgments. Reinforcing these often are the cultural survivals of different national origin groups, going back to the lives of their forebears in the country of their origin. In still other cases there are differences in social prestige between the persons making an inter-faith marriage, thus adding another dimension to the resulting problems. There is, however, an individual aspect to all of this. Much depends upon the attitudes of the persons marrying towards religion, marriage and family.

It is obvious, then, that each inter-faith marriage is unique, differing in some respects from every other one. Each represents its own distinctive combination of cultural values, traditional attachments, and prestige position of two persons. Each represents the union of the ways in which the matrimonial mates refract their religious backgrounds. Finally, each inter-faith marriage is unique because every marriage, regardless of religious factors, is unique. For every marriage brings together two different persons, each with their own distinctive array of personal traits and characteristics.

4

Conversion, Assimilation and Reconciliation

Inter-religion marriage in the broader sense has been explained as the linkage of two people with different cultural and behavioural norms and backgrounds grounded or based on religious, racial, or ethnic differences. Inter-marriage, a form of exogamy, is a marriage between members of different groups or marriage outside one's social group. Inter-faith marriage typically connotes a marriage in which both partners remain adherents to their distinct religion and as such it is distinct from concepts of religious conversion, religious assimilation, cultural assimilation, religious disaffiliation and apostasy.

But it also seems clear that marriage is not normally about the prospective spouse and their independent desire to marry. Family and kinship groups, lineages, economic and political interests, social organisation, gender relations, are all part of the phenomenon. Since marriage is located at the intersection of personal, social, political, economic, legal and communal relationships, its occurrence across group lines, whether of caste, class, religion, or race, brings at least two sets of norms, aspirations about social relations together, in the private as well as the public domain.

Studies of inter-religion marriages in general tend to locate this practice in the broader context of inter-group relations, seeing it as testing social boundaries. Inter-religion marriages raise questions about whether insiders and outsiders are willing to accept each other in a long lasting, exclusive, and largely non-hierarchical relationship. Seen in this light, inter-religion marriages are a fundamentally important 'measure of social distance and structural assimilation.' Consequently, under conditions of social flux, the social, political and religious implications of individuals who marry across frontiers become particularly visible when communities feel that their resources are at risk, belief systems are under attack and security is at stake. It is therefore important to emphasise the contextual nature of how the spouse, and their wider families, kin, and communities, understand and engage in inter-religious marriages.

Inter-religious marriages have implications not only for the couple themselves but on the linkages of larger family and lineage groups as well. The consequences of the marriage not only affect the family but also future generations. Inter-religious marriages are very uncommon in India and being so rare and taken for granted. Still there is a lack of perspective on it. The nature and dynamics of inter-religion marriages provides insights into the understanding of religion, race, and ethnic group relationships as they operate both within and between societies. Hence there arise various questions about the sociological implications of the current trend of inter-religion marriages in India. Should we call it a pattern? It is clear that the imbalance of the cultures, psychological and societal ethos created has its significant ramifications upon inter-religion spouses. The anchoring question remains on the fate of women who enter such marriages and what is their pattern of adjustment in the newly embraced cultural, social and religious set up? What is the woman's inner thought process? The worth pondering and perhaps worth assessing aspect is whether there is a deeply embedded remorse or sense of guilt or pain of denunciating her near and dear ones? What is the fate of her feeling of not being able to perform the ceremonies of her marriage with her parents and relatives, as inter-religion marriages are seldom cermonised with pomp and show in the Indian social set up? What is the state of treatment meted out to such women by the in-laws and is she accepted wholeheartedly or treated as a mistake or sin on the part of their son? What remains her religious identity and in case of conversion, what is her assimilative pattern? Are such conversions just a condition to undergo such marriages? Also do such women after conversion diligently follow the adopted religion or is there a superficial feeling of adherence to a new faith? What enables this conversion to survive and in case of no conversions, what remains the pattern of adjustment and faith pattern of spouses?

The mixed religious marriages historically have been an ideological dilemma as well as a threat to the different religious groups. It has been a dilemma because each religion espouses the doctrine of brotherly love and acceptance of others. But such a doctrine, when carried to its logical conclusion of marriages creates a peculiar situation. The abandoning of one's religious faith, in order to accept another in marriage, constitutes a threat to the organised religious bodies, since it means an eventual loss of followers. The couple attempts to resolve their differences over religion by one of the spouses accepting the faith of the other, usually before the marriage ceremony. Thus, an important characteristic of inter-religion marriages is the phenomenon of conversion and the loss of religious identity for that partner. From a sample of fifty couples in this study, thirty-six had chosen conversion. But this should not lead one to believe that those who are not converted have total religious independence. Even amongst the non-converted, one of the spouses has to accept the other's religion. This is in a sense a sort of disguised conversion.

'I have converted and do not practise any rituals regularly. I am religious. My husband is also religious. I go to the *mandir* (House of worship for Hindus) with my natal family. I have faith in God. We live together and are both religious', says Sarita who became Khalida after marriage.

However, marriage practices, beliefs and rules vary widely

by religion, caste and community. Marriage arrangements constitute a key site for distinguishing groups from one another, preserving lineage, and in consolidating and maintaining rank. Endogamous marriages are to be arranged by elders of the family to maintain purity of caste and preserve social status. Indeed distinctions of purity and impurity are considered central to caste identities among Hindus. This purity is literally found in blood, and can be altered, polluted by contact with less pure people. 'Inter-caste marriages or affairs produce relatively impure progeny......A child inherits whatever purity is contained in parental blood. Line preserving liaisons occur between persons from the same group (jati)', Harlan and Court (1995: 6). Additionally, the marriage between a higher caste woman with a lower caste man is considered *pratiloma* or against the grain, and violating the very structure of society, resulting in offspring who are considered impure, with women's purity critical to the maintenance of the family's social status and rank.

From a sociological perspective, it can be argued that when lineage became patriarchal, women are viewed as the ones who adulterate the race by marrying men from unacceptable groups. The same concern began to be expressed in religious terms for those communities where religion was either closely associated with ethnicity, or became a strong bond among believers. The control of women and their reproductive functions continued throughout history, whether justified in religious, ideological or other terms. In this way, marriage has always been a public institution, a matter of central importance to social policy, and foundation of citizenship and the state.

In a patrilocal system, the bride moves into her husband's household after the marriage and is expected to adjust to the customs and traditions of the husband's family. In an inter-religion marriage, when she shifts to her in-laws' family, especially joint family, she comes across different culture, food habits, dressing norms, lifestyle and religious rituals which she is expected to follow. To assimilate into her husband's religion, culture and lifestyle she converts. Conversion for the sake of acceptance by in-laws seems an important consideration. Another important reason is the desire for adjustment in married life. For Rekha Kapoor now Nafisa Begum, 'I think conversion is very helpful for acceptance in a different religion by the in-laws. The decision to convert was taken because I was mentally prepared as I knew that I have to lose something to get something. For marriage of my own choice I have to lose my religion.' The respondents who convert believe that conversion would pave the way to parental approval, which would subsequently lead to harmonious relations. Renuka Khan also responded in agreement with Nafisa stating that, 'Conversion is important if one wants to please everyone'. For Anjana Sharma now Rukhsana Ali, 'conversion is very important. My mother-inlaw told me that if I stand in two boats then I can't be loyal to anyone. I can't do puja neither be loyal to Islam because there is no *Mabood* except Allah. Then how can I perform both, puja as well as namaz?'

As a matter of fact, some do this as a superficial or nominal act. For Rachna Chauhan, 'I am still more of a Hindu at heart and say my own prayers. I do puja but people don't know. Even my children don't know. I am sure that if my in-laws come to know about this then they won't accept me. Therefore, I secretly do puja and openly show that I follow Islam. However that does not mean that I do not have faith in Islam. I am open to both religions. Even my husband is fine with my following Hinduism provided that my original faith stays hidden from the the children as well as neighbours'. Another respondent replied in the same vein. For Sanjana Rawat now Zoya Khan, 'sometimes I wonder why I have converted, because I am not following any ritual. I have converted for the sake of nikah only.'

Conversion to the spouse's faith may be voluntary or forced. The spouse who gets converted voluntarily desires to bridge the gap of religious differences, so that religious disagreements could be avoided and specific religious conflicts could be prevented. 'I try to offer namaz but not regularly. Now I am learning what Islam is. But when my husband forces me it suffocates me. I accept that Islam is a very good religion. But some people make it complicated', said Nirja Joshi. There is an emotional side to conversion. Some of the female respondents had gained peace of mind by converting to their spouse's faith. 'I chose conversion as it made my husband and his family happy. I have thus eliminated one cause of conflict and unhappiness from our marriage', said Koyal Sharma now Nagma Alam.

Imran who married Sujata now Rehana says, 'I think that conversion is important as it helps a girl to get her marriage and relationship approved before in-laws. We met in 1996 and after one year we decided to marry. Pertaining to conversion, I put a condition to her that she must have faith in this religion and not as a compulsion. It should be accepted willingly from the heart'. He further narrates, 'from the Islamic point of view, conversion of the wife is necessary and is considered as *swaab*, a good deed.'

Conversion has twin features of one spouse losing his/her initial religious identity, and the children are brought up in the religion which both parents follow. Conversion has been given greater emphasis in case of such marriages.

One of the partners converts to the other's religion for the sake of their relationship and usually women have to convert to the husband's religion. In most cases since the girls were Hindus and the boys were Muslims, it was the girls who converted to Islam and took on the lifestyle of their husband's family. But in a few cases Muslim boys converted to Hinduism at the time of marriage. Conversion without any real love for the religion may not bring harmony in the family. A male's experience is illustrative: 'I have become a Hindu so that my wife's people would accept us, but I am just not interested in practising that religion. I feel half the feasts are meaningless. My spouse has tried her best to seek my participation, but my lack of enthusiasm angers her'. Similarly Sanjana, now Zoya, says, 'I don't practise any ritual. I have converted but I don't know anything about Islam. This is because my husband does not expect me to offer namaz and perform any ritual. He also does not practise any ritual, I respect all religions. When I listen to *Azan* Muslim call for prayer, I cover my head out of respect.'

Conversion by choice may often be before marriage and in some cases even after the actual marriage ceremony is over. When the natal family of the respondent was strongly opposed to the inter-religious marriage and rejected all proposals of reconciliation, there was a tendency of accepting the spouse's religion on the part of the respondent. Those who are converted after the marriage have, to some extent, accepted the new religion. Their conversion is believed to be motivated by belief in the new faith. 'In my home, there was no religious atmosphere. Thus after marriage, I have come to know what religion is and I have gained knowledge too. This is the first time I am practising rituals and following any religion. Hence, I never faced any problem. Initially, I had a problem because I did not do anything before. But now I am used to doing all the rituals', Rekha Kapoor now Nafisa Begum.

Conversion means a fund of personal organisation, a new identity and a new alignment with a religious group. In the conversion of people to new doctrines other than their own, the newly accepted ideas often undergo considerable change. The chief reason for conversion as analysed in our case studies is that many respondents found conversion to Islam an easy and quick option to get married. In India there is the Special Marriage Act 1954, but couples who did not have any societal support found it very difficult to marry under this act. Marrying under law can be legal but acceptance is not guaranteed.

The other reason of conversion after marriage was to give the children a uniform religious background so that they would be well received socially and not be the targets of any kind of ridicule, gossip or ostracism. Conversion is mostly deemed by couples and parents of men who enter such unions as very important to avoid a confused identity of children and for the holistic well-being and stability of the relationship. For Ishaq Husain, 'I think that conversion is necessary and important from the Islamic point of view. For the sake of children, if the father practises his religion and the mother practises her religion, it confuses them.' For the father of Ishaq Husain, Saiyed Sajid Husain, 'I don't think that if each spouse follows his or her religion marriage can be successful. It creates confusion for children as the couple cannot maintain a healthy relationship'. For, the children born may be brought up in the other spouse's faith. For this very reason, many couples prefer a conversion at the time of marriage.

There have been enough differences among the teachings of the Hindu and Muslim faith to make inter-faith marriages one of the most difficult types of mixed marriages. There is no conversion in Hinduism. The *Arya Samaj* Hindu Reform movement introduced the *Shuddhi Karan* purification ceremony which was both a reaction and considered move against the proselytising creed of both Islam and Christianity, which by their conversion, had considerably depleted the number of Hindus. The Shuddhi soon assumed the form of a religious-cum-political movement and it became a major plank of the militant Hindu nationalism. This has set a trend of conversions of non-Hindus to Hinduism.

The two faiths oppose these marriages for various reasons, the most important one being the loss of new members to the religious group. Islam is based on conversion and non-Muslims who prefer a Muslim marriage ceremony are converted by a *Qazi*. The scriptures say in no uncertain terms that there can be no marriage between a believer and a non-believer. 'I think that conversion is very important. Without conversion, one can't do nikah. And I think that for the sake of children it is better to follow the same religion', Sujata now Rehana.

For some people, conversion may not be all that effective. 'When a girl comes to a different religion, it is harder for her. This is because she always tries to please the family members. But after some time she has to follow the religion of the husband.

'In the beginning, when a girl converts she finds that things are going in her favour, but after sometime she faces many problems which are not bearable. Thus I think that conversion is not necessary for getting the acceptance of the in-laws', Ambika Zaidi.

Those couples, who had been married for more than five years, said that they had gradually cultivated a taste for each other's food. The vegetarians and non-vegetarians had resolved their differences after the initial inconvenience. In most cases, the couples who had inter-religion marriages said that there was a basic change in their food habits after their marriage, especially in the case of women. The girls in any case were expected to take over the lifestyle of their husband's family and most girls accepted that as a 'package deal'. But in case the boy was converted to the religion of his wife, whether Hindu or Muslim, there was very little change in his life. Men continued to practise their earlier lifestyle. This includes non-vegetarian food, 'I bring *halal,* and I inform my in-laws that this is halal, and they should choose if they want to have this , since I don't buy *jhatka* meat (animal killed as per Sikh rituals). They have no problem', Zahid married to Sikh female Kamaljeet. Even acceptance of beef, which is forbidden to Hindus, is seen as a test for the girl who converts to Islam. 'I have not started eating beef. I am offering namaz and follow all other rituals. But privately I can't accept eating beef. I have no objection if my husband does so', says Rajni, now Reshma.

In Indian weddings, the change mostly comes from the wife's side. The changes begin from food habits. In a number of cases, women who were vegetarian before marriage gradually became non-vegetarian. For Seema now Rehana, 'after marriage my food habits have changed. I started eating non-vegetarian food and also started preparing biryani and paya, which I personally like very much.'

For Leela Saiyed, 'I am now non-vegetarian. After my marriage my food habits have changed. Members of my family were vegetarians and had different kinds of food. After my marriage, I learnt to make kababs, biryani, etc.' However, it was a slow and difficult process to adopt Muslim food habits because not only are Muslims generally non-vegetarian but their style of cooking, i.e. Mughal cuisine, is more spicy and rich in terms of oils used, and therefore more difficult to digest. It takes time for women to be able to adjust to the new food habits, especially if they have been vegetarian before marriage. Again beef is cooked only in Muslim homes especially in the lower middle class families. For Bhawna Kumari now Samira, 'my food habits changed but not much. I can't eat beef but I make beef for my husband and son. Before my marriage I was vegetarian but now I eat chicken and mutton.' In another case Rajnish Kumar, husband of Fatima, comments, 'I am pure vegetarian. But my wife and son are non-vegetarian. They make non-vegetarian food. I also bring chicken and mutton for them. After marriage I have not changed my food habits.'

The non-vegetarian food for upper middle class Muslims includes only mutton, chicken and fish. But they are not averse to the idea of eating beef. For Hindus, the cow is considered a sacred animal even amongst non-vegetarians. Hindus cannot reconcile themselves to eating beef just as Muslims about eating pork. Many Hindu men are non-vegetarian but women still continue to be vegetarian. In patriarachy, it is natural for the family of the husband to expect that the woman will adjust to the food habits of the husband's family which includes eating non-vegetarian food. If conversion has taken place, expectations from the Hindu girl are even greater. For Nirja Joshi, 'I feel suffocated when my husband tells me to try non-vegetarian food. It is easier for him to think that I will give up my religious norms. But it is simply not possible.

Many respondents who were vegetarians maintained their particular food habits even after an inter-religious marriage and the acceptance of a non-vegetarian spouse. The respondents, who stayed in joint households, said that the spouse had to get used to the type of food cooked in these homes. All these adjustments were, however, made even though food habits reflect certain basic religious notions.

Quite a few vegetarians were married to non-vegetarians. It should be taken into account that households in India follow a style of cooking which may vary from religion to religion. The Muslims are non-vegetarians and have a totally different way of cooking. The utensils used for cooking are different in the Hindu and Muslim homes.

As time passes, the food habits of the couples and the members of the entire family undergo subtle changes. Not only do vegetables gradually increase in the menu but even the style of cooking food undergoes a change. The total effect of inter-religion marriages on the food habits is one which becomes an amalgam of Hindu-Muslim food habits perhaps the best of both cuisines.

Assimilation covered all kinds of interpersonal relationships. The female respondents felt that one way of achieving this was by constantly giving in to the other relatives. That is, not opposing their views, by acquiescing constantly.

Either due to the domination of one partner or the voluntary acceptance by the other partner—the couple made their adjustments in food habits. Common items acceptable to both were prepared.

Even clothing undergoes some changes, especially in the initial phase of the marriage and it is the woman who is expected to accept the dress code followed by her husband's family. For Sarita Agnihotri now Sakina Khanam, 'I often wear suits but I like to wear saris too. But my husband doesn't like it. Though he buys me saris he does not like them. Thus I wear saris for parties only. Sometime the sari becomes the cause of household conflict'.

If the husband's family belongs to a lower middle class income group, then, the chances are that the women may even start wearing burqas or hijabs. At times it is observed that the new converts are stronger adherents to their new faith.

For Babita Arora now Farhana Afreen, 'my family knew that I got married to a Muslim boy. After marriage I started wearing a burqa. My family didn't like it. They kept asking me whether I was comfortable or not. I assured them that I was very comfortable. When I couldn't convince them eventually, I stopped going there. I can't move one step without a burqa'.

'I don't wear sari. I only wear suits. Before marriage I wore jeans and all types of outfits', one of the respondents mentioned. For Sujata now Rehana, 'The pattern of dressing has also changed. Before marriage I wore skirts and never used a dupatta but now I wear only suits and also wear *niqab*.'

If the couple is highly educated, economically sound and living away from the joint family, in their own independent homes, there may not be much change in the lifestyle either in food or in dress. For one respondent, Sheena Dikshit now Shama, 'when I stay here I wore jeans all the time, but when I go to my in-laws' house, I don't wear Western attire.' Hindu girls wore a *bindi* as a fashion. But in case a Hindu girl who was married to a Muslim wore a *bindi* (a mark on the forhead worn by generally Hindu women), it would be seen with great suspicion and criticism. It would be viewed as an assertion of her Hindu identity. Even if there was no restriction from the husband and in-laws, women who were married to Muslim males hesitated and avoided using bindis or sindoor. The important concern in their minds was to prove their allegiance or devotion towards their newly adopted religion. Jasmeet said, 'no one has stopped me from wearing nail polish and bindis. In fact before marriage I had a large collection of bindis but now I feel hesitant to wear nail polish, bindi or *mangalsutra*', (a necklace worn by married Hindu women), but Muslim women, when they got married to Hindu men, wore the *bindi* quite religiously. Sanjana Rawat now Zoya Khan had no restrictions. She stated, 'I am not a religious person. I don't apply *sindoor* (a mark of a married women in Hinduism) and *bindi* because I don't like such things. If I like them, I would do so because there is no restriction.' There is another side of the coin. A mother of the girl, who married a Muslim and converted, praised the leniency of her daughter's in-laws. For Nafisa Begum's mother, 'my daughter's in-laws don't restrict her from doing anything. She is free to go anywhere. We also gave her freedom but we don't like her to be outside till late at night. We want the girls to know their limitations and my daughter knows her limitations. Her mother-inlaw is so advanced that she allows my daughter to wear sleeveless blouses and suits. She says at this age you can wear such clothes. One can't wear these when one becomes old.'

The change in the lifestyle extends to the celebration of religious festivals. Since inter-religion unions bring together partners from two different cultures, bi-culturism becomes the norm. Thus the couple tend to observe each other's festivals. Again female respondents said that when they stayed with their in-laws, they had to make a lot of adjustments. 'We don't celebrate Holi and Diwali here since my locality is Muslim-dominant. We don't go to my parents' house during Holi because my husband and I also do not like it much. But during Diwali, we go to my parents' house and enjoy ourselves there, ' said Jaya now Nagma.

The festivals of both religions were celebrated and it was observed that mostly the women who had converted did not take part in the rituals of thier 'natal' religion. In cases where the couples visited the women's parental home it was usually to be present in the house at the time of celebration. 'I have faith in all religions. I celebrate all festivals including Eid. I don't celebrate Holi and Diwali here. At my parents' house I can celebrate but I do not participate in puja', says Reshma.

If the woman takes part in the rituals she may perform the ritual on behalf of her husband also. 'We are not averse to any religion. We participate in festivals of both religions. He participates in my festivals but he does not perform puja. During Diwali we do aarti and I do puja on his behalf, ' says Surjana.

The woman might frequently visit her parental house, to celebrate a festival, as she is aware that her presence there will make her natal family happy in spite of the fact that she does not want to take part in the rituals. 'It is not possible to celebrate Holi and Diwali festivals here. But even when I go to my brother's house, I do not wish to celebrate. However my brother is happy if I take part in festivals and that is only important for me. Otherwise, I don't do puja', said Rehana. Kamljeet and Zahid celebrate festivals without rituals. 'We do not celebrate festivals as such, but during Eid and Diwali we invite our friends and visit their homes. We also distribute sweets.'

In Indian society, religion and caste are very important factors specially at the time of birth, marriage and death. These rites to passage continue to be arranged according to caste rituals. Another important dilemma couples of inter-religion marriages face is about their death rituals as they are guided by the ascribed status of the individuals. Many respondents were of the view that after conversion their death rituals should be according to their new religion, but there were couples who felt otherwise. 'Preferably my death ritual should be electrical cremation or donation of my body to medical institutes. Through this somebody could be helped', said Leela Saiyed.

Reconciliation

Those parents, who had unsuccessfully tried to dissuade their children from a mixed marriage, had invariably been angered by the couple's doggedness to go ahead. Some of these angered parents had retaliated by not maintaining any social contact with the couple. For one respondent Preeti, 'my in-laws were shocked but my parents were shattered because they had faith and confidence in me, which I had broken. I had cheated them which is why there is still some anger. There is interaction with my parents but they do not talk to me the way they interacted with me earlier.' For another respondent, Sunena now Zehra, 'I have got married on 19th November but I did not disclose my marriage to my parents. After three months, I disclosed my marriage. During that period we were hunting for a home and searching for the necessary items. I would have told about my marriage to my father but one day he randomly said that except for a Muslim, I could marry anybody. I was so scared that I had to conceal this information from him. The day my parents came to know about my marriage, they wanted to kill both of us.' Yet in many cases the couple was finally successful in softening the parental attitude to the mixed marriage and in winning their goodwill. Parental love and affection, which got a sudden serious setback for some time, regained full force, and reconciliation took place. The time of reconciliation, however, was not uniform, nor are the reasons same in all cases. Similarly, various factors had played their role in this process of reconciliation.

As far as the parents of inter-religion couples were concerned it emerged very clearly that whether the woman was a Hindu or a Muslim, the parents of the woman were more opposed to the marriage compared to the parents of the boy. For Bhawna now Samira, 'my parents tried to convince me to leave him after my marriage. They wanted me to divorce him and start my life again. They wanted me to forget everything. For me, they wanted to leave this place and go to an unknown place where we would start our life again.' Bhawna's parents went to the extent of disowning their daughter. Sometimes the mother reconciled herself to the marriage of her daughter by saying that it was pre-ordained or it was destiny. But the father of the woman found it more difficult to accept the marriage if his daughter had got married to a person of her own choice and also someone belonging to a different religious community. It is he who had to face the world and he felt it was a personal loss, humiliation, loss of honour and a very traumatic experience for him. In one case, Rajani now Reshma's parents accepted, her decision to marry her Muslim neighbour after initial opposition. But her father, a community leader, continues to be ostracised by his brothers and his community after the marriage. In another case, the agony of the marriage was so great that the father could never reconcile himself to his daughter's marriage to a Muslim and he was mentally wrecked. Consequently, he passed away. The mother was willing to reconcile herself to the marriage but, because of pressure from her husband and other close relatives could not express her willingness to reconcile herself to the marriage specially when there were younger children who were still to be married. 'My parents came to know about my marriage after I got married. Thus they could not prevent it. But they tried their best to convince me to discard our marriage. Their only problem was why I had married a Muslim boy. When they could not succeed to prove that our marriage was wrong they presseurised us to dissolve it'. said Manjari now Noor, wife of Md. Alam.

The family holds special importance at the time of

marriage. Even today it becomes extremely difficult for the parents to find suitable brides and bridegrooms for their younger children if one of their children especially a daughter marries outside their religious community. In such cases, the problem of finding suitable mate for younger siblings becomes more challanging if it is the inter-religion marriage of women. For Sushma, 'my parents have not reconciled and they have not disclosed to their relatives that I am married to a Muslim man. My marriage has deeply affected my family and relatives. They know that I had a love marriage. My sister also told her in-laws that I had a court marriage and she mentioned that my husband's name is Neeraj. They avoid inviting me to any marriage, social occasions or any festivals. This is because they fear that other people would come to know about my marriage.'

Some parents have even persuaded their daughters to go abroad after marriage if they have got married outside their community. That seems to be an easy escape from the stark criticism they would have to face from the society. They can say that their daughter has gone abroad and they do not know whether their daughter has got married or not and to whom she has got married to. In some cases, when the parents could afford it they even send their daughter abroad to settle down there in order to save themselves from the agony and trauma of their daughter's marriage into another religious community. The fear of social ostracism is so high that many females have their natal families, parents and siblings completely severed their ties with them. This has become the major reason of pain and loss of social capital for them. There also lies a deep sense of guilt and remorse among women especially who have converted to their husband's religion for they feel a loss of religious identity, mostly disowned by parents and hardly anyone from the parental side to visit and care for after entering such marriages. For Manjari now Noor, wife of Md. Alam, 'initially, the relationship with my in-laws was not good but now it is good. But I have still no contact with my parents. I am in touch only with my *Bhabi* (sister-in-law).'

The interviews conducted with the parents revealed that the mother of the daughter who had an inter-religion marriage was more willing to be interviewed than the father. Most fathers refused to talk about their daughter's marriage. They said that they have nothing to do with their daughters' marriages and they do not want to talk about the marriage. Therefore, very few interviews could be conducted with the fathers of women in inter-religion marriages. In a few cases, we could not contact the parents because the 'shame or the loss of honour' for the parents of the girls was so great that it would have been unethical on our part to subject them to the pain of the interview. Even the mothers who were willing to be interviewed were too apprehensive to talk to us because they did not want to annoy their husbands.

It is not that there was complete rejection of such daughters by the parents but in many cases we found that the parental love forced parents for reconciliation with their daughters. 'In my opinion parents can't do anything in this matter. This is because at that time children do not care about parents. They are so much in love that they can't see anything else. Thus it is better to be with them', Rekha now Nafisa's father, Mahesh Singh.

Reshma's parents supported her. 'My parents are very close to me. They knew that if I have chosen someone then he would be good. My parents knew my husband very well. Thus they accepted him. In fact they went to my in- laws to convince them and they succeeded'. Whereas another respondent Sarita Agnihotri, now Sakina Khanam, thought parental support is essential, 'I think that in any marriage whether it is inter- faith marriage or intra-faith marriages, parents' approval is very important. This is because when parents don't approve, girls have to face many problems. If parents approve then one does not have to hide and not face so many problems, which we have faced'.

At times, the parents support the inter-religion marriage of their daughter but are unable express their support overtly due to vehement opposition of their other family members. For

Sanjana now Zoya, 'earlier my parents were not happy with my marriage. But when they came to know my husband cares for me so much they were very happy. But they can't show it and invite me to their house. This is because my brother is very much against my marriage as he is very conservative. He cannot accept a Muslim brother-in-law. When my parents planned to visit my house he tried to commit suicide. Thus my parents can not express their joy. They meet me outside.'

It has been observed in our study that the wife's family finds it more difficult to accept the son-in-law who belongs to a different religious community and more so if he is a Muslim. Amjad Husain married to Bhawana said, 'my in-laws' family had a problem in accepting me as their son-in-law. We had no contact until five months when after they called her and invited her to their house. As for accepting me as their son-in-law, they took three years. But they still do not like me.'

As already noted, when the parents are against a mixed marriage the brothers and sisters too are generally against the marriage. In a few cases, however, brothers and sisters were broad-minded and they tried to convince the parents. Sometimes brothers of the girl are very helpful. For Rajni now Reshma, 'there is no problem in such a marriage. My brother always gives me something whenever I go to his house. My husband does not ask for anything.' In some cases although they disliked their parents' hostility, they could not do much in the matter except give their secret support. Relatives also could not give any effective help once the parents were known to be dead set against a mixed marriage. Only the intimate friends helped during such difficulties.

The case with the boy's parents was different. They reconciled themselves to the marriage more easily even if they were initially reluctant because they did not want to lose their son. Most parents of the boys said they accepted the marriage of their son to the girl of his choice even if she belonged to a different religious community as they did not want to lose their son. The mothers, for example, were sure that if they did not accept her son's marriage he would take his wife away and refuse to meet them. In any case they had nothing to lose. In fact they had gained because there was an addition to the family and the gain was even more if the girl had agreed to convert to their religion. Also, most mothers-in-law of such women seemed to be very happy with their daughters-in-law from other religion as they made special efforts and took greater care of the family as compared to other daughters-in-law who came from the same religious community. For Riyaz-ud-din's mother, 'my relationship with my daughter–in-law is cordial. She cares for me.' The couple works more for the family of the in-laws to gain "acceptance" for themselves and for their children. Such converted daughters-in-law performed *roza, namaz,* and read the Quran more seriously, sincerely and with greater devotion. Both the mothers-in-law and fathers-in-law accepted them more readily. For Zubair Alam's father, Zeeshan-ur-Zafar, 'I was worried initially and wondered what would happen to my younger generation. I am a very religious person. I cannot compromise with my religion but the way my daughter-in-law has adjusted to my family, it is praiseworthy. I am very happy with her.' Most parents-in-law of Hindu women, expressed their happiness over the marriages of their sons even if in the initial phase of their marriages there was some hostility and strong opposition.

Inter-religion marriages come up with greater reconciliation. The conversion is taken as a prerequisite especially when girls marry Muslim boys. The assimilation and reconciliation is difficult for women who enter such marriages. One of the cases, Dr Wahab says, 'with the passage of time all approved our marriage'. Relatives were happy that the bride converted to Islam. He says, 'My wife learnt to cook Muslim cuisine'.

'I think that conversion is very important because if she does not convert, it would affect her life and also their children. We want our daughter-in-law to follow our religion so it helps in understanding and maintaining a healthy relationship, it also brings happy moments for both the family as well as to the spouse', says Iffat Begum. It depicts how conversion is deemed important and serves as a positive factor for acceptance of the girl by the in-laws. She has to comply with the culture and adjust herself even to food habits. The factor of assimilation is characterised by adjusting to new food habits, compromising with her religious faith, dress pattern and above all conversion.

They also feel a great pain to adopt cultural norms and values of the new life pattern. They feel problems in adjustment like food pattern, dress pattern, way of talking or behaving happens on a routine basis. 'Suddenly I did not start eating non-vegetarian food. It was after eight months of our marriage I started eating it. Once I was ill, my husband prepared a dish for me. It was very tasty. Later on I came to know that it was non-vegetarian, says Suchita, now Neelofer Alam, wife of Nusrat Alam. She further adds, 'within the same religion marriage is more successful and if someone would come to take my suggestion, I will not suggest inter-religion marriage, I tell them to marry within their own religion'.

Our study reveals that in most cases where conversion had taken place, the marriage was more easily acceptable to the husband's family. But, the girl's family often became more distanced from their daughter after the marriage of the daughter especially if she was converted to Islam. But, where a registered marriage had taken place the resentment from the husband's parents persisted over a longer period of time. The marriage was more acceptable to the parents of the bride if a registered marriage had taken place. On the other hand as mentioned above, the parents of the boy agreed to the marriage and accepted it more readily if conversion of the girl had taken place. It is precisely to win the support of the boy's family with whom she had to live and interact for the rest of her life. There, conversion was seen as an easy way to adapt to the family of in-laws. Family support is, therefore, one of the main issues in inter-religion marriages. The children would be better adjusted and happier and contribute more to the secular ethos of the society if their respective families and society at large were to support them. And, there would be many more such marriages if parents and close relatives provided the necessary social support which they provide to marriages within the caste and within the religious community.

But it may not be wrong to argue that such marriages prove to be more of a sacrifice for women than men. Adjustments, new socialisation and adherence to norms and values, denouncing a previous lifestyle and likes and dislikes for the sake of absorption in the new relationship. The most important factor of conversion thereby, denouncing religious faith, losing name, identity, relationship, family and what not for the sake of husbands' acceptance, children's rights socialisation and chaos-free upbringing, acceptance among in-laws, total exit from her own community and society. Women are always at the lower end and compromising from the beginning till the end. Marital adjustments are often seriously affected by conflicting concepts of the role of the husband or wife. The wife, who, because of her conditioning and socialisation has imbibed patriarchal values, makes an effort to assimilate into the family of her husband. And with this training and socialisation, the wife of an inter-religion marriage, usually converts to the husband's religion to assimilate in her in-laws' culture and lifestyle, especially if she is staying in a joint family. She might be following a new religion but she doesn't forget her previous religion. And she is the person who experiences that by changing a religion a person does not change and realises that any religion cannot be good or bad. It is the individual who is good or bad and his deeds affect the image of his/her religion in the eyes of the world. Therefore the prejudices pertaining to a certain religion is a very generalised image of a person in the eyes of the other. So when the wife of an inter-religion marriage, after internalising this concept interacts with people, she is subconsciously treating people on the basis of their deeds and not on the prejudicial image of the religion of those persons. She, also by her behaviour, influences her husband by such values. And logically, she socialises her children with these values which incidentally have nothing to do with the question that their children should follow which religion. So inter-religion marriages might lead to conversion, assimilation of one of the spouses, it promotes multiculturalism and tolerance for the other religions. In the society, when xenophobia and religious intolerance is spreading like cancer, inter-religion marriages spreads the message of religious tolerance and multiculturalism which is essentially due to the union of two individual with different cultural backgrounds. These type of families strengthen the traditions of composite culture. Our study has reflected that such unions have assimilative tendencies which in a way strengthen the secular ethos of multicultural societies.

5

Socialisation of Children in Inter-Religion Marriages

The impact of inter-religion marriages in terms of intensity and a long-term effect is most severely felt by the children. The socialisation pattern of children has secular and religious implications. Of course, much depends on the socio-economic background of the parents, their education and the locality or neighbourhood in which they live. It has been much argued that children born out of such marriages develop a confused identity, be it religious or cultural adherence. It has been found that in the majority of cases women have converted to their husband's faith. Hence both the partners follow the same religion and socialise their children in the same culture. However, the socialisation of an individual in a particular culture has its deep impact. Even though after conversion it is very difficult to forget and unlearn the previous lifestyle. Also in cases where the couple is either secular or following their respective religion, children mostly follow their father's faith. It is also observed that children of such couples are not confused about their religious status. 'I have not faced any confusion about my religious status because both my father and mother follow the same religion. My mother is a very religious lady and she offers namaz regularly', said Ishaq Husain's daughter, Ayesha Hasan. 'I am very happy that my mother has converted' said, daughter of Koyal Sharma. Among

Muslims, the existence of the institution of *Ustani-Shagird* (lady teacher and student/discipline) where a child (especially a girl child) is given into the custody of an *ustani* who not only imparts religious education including the recitation of the Quran but also socialize, the child into the culture of the Muslims, e.g. maintaining purdah from strangers, showing respect to elders etc. The boys between the age group of 6-10 years are preferably sent to a nearby masjid or madarsa where a similar training in religious education takes place for them.

Many socio-economic variables have a deep impact on the adjustment patterns of children whose parents have had inter-religion marriages. If the father is a Muslim and the family lives in a Muslim-dominated area, the children are expected to adapt themselves to the culture, traditions and religion of the Muslim community. But, if the child is exposed to Hindu culture, the acceptance of Hindu tradition would be greater.

The case studies reveal that the children of inter-religion marriages experience loss of identity when they are young and till the time that they understand the intricacies of relationships and how these marriages have enriched their own lives. 'My son likes both the religions as we have given him a secular outlook. When he was a child he did not know his identity. When he was studying in the nursery class, he realised that he is Muslim and he identified this through his name, ' said Leela Saiyed. When they grow up they understand what values they have imbibed because of the inter-religion marriage of their parents and start appreciating and taking pride in this fact. They were grateful for being the children of such couples who have given them such secular values and such a broad and wide perspective. They have learnt to respect all religions and human beings irrespective of their ideologies. Fatima's son was influenced by his parents inter-religion marriage he said, 'my parents have always taught me to give importance to values and culture, and to be a good and honest human being and respect relatives. There is a supernatural power and I have faith in him. I will teach these things to my children. I will not force my children to follow any particular religion, they can follow what they want.'

Values Inherited by Children in Mixed Marriages

The couple who had an inter-religion marriage have society already against them but it is their children who bear the brunt of societal opposition if they are not protected. The couple tries to give secular socialisation to their children so as to mitigate the difference between them and the children of intra-religion marriage and make them homogeneous in the society. This secular socialisation is related to the language the child should learn, the type of food the child should be given, the school the child should attend and so on.

Therefore the important question that arises is about the state of the children born out of an inter-religion marriages. How are children brought up? Do they always follow patriarchal culture? What faith do they adhere to? Is it always the father's faith? Are they aware of the inter-religion marriage of their parents or do the parents hide it treating it as a stigma to reveal it to their kids?

The responses were candid regarding the secular areas of socialisation and there was considerable agreement on these matters. It has been found in our study that the customs followed in most of the households have a dual character and considerable numbers of children accept such dual customs. Those who do not are very few and some of them are unable to accept these customs because the children concerned are too young to express, appreciate or protest. The respondents said that most of the customs pertained to the celebration of festivals. Children were happy to receive gifts, good clothes and enjoyed good food on these special occasions. One child aged 12 responded, 'I feel very happy, that I have relatives from both communities and it gives me the opportunity to celebrate all the festivals.' Likewise for Iqbal, son of Amjad and Bhawana/Samira said, 'my parents follow the same religion. So we don't see any confusion in our house. We follow Islam. I know that my mother previously followed Hinduism. But this does not bother us. Because now I see that she tells us to offer namaz and also instructs us to read the Quran. When we go to our *Nani*'s house, we respect their culture. When *Mousi* (mother's sister) and *Maama* (mother's brother) go to the *mandir*, we also go along with them not to pray, but only for knowledge. I went to the *mandir* with my mother, father and aunt. My aunt did puja and we observed her. I also ate the *prashad* (mixture of wheat and sugar offered to diety) offered at the *puja*. We have in-depth knowledge about both religions. I like both festivals. We do not perform puja at Diwali. We enjoy it. I like Eid, Diwali and Holi. I celebrate Diwali and Holi but I like Eid more than any other festival. I decorate my *Nani's* (maternal grand mother) house with candles and we burst crackers. During Holi we put colours on people who come to our house.' Iqbal further says, 'I know who Ram is, and what is the Ramayana. Ram is a God for Hindus. Hindus worship and read the Ramayana every day like we read the Quran every day. The Ramayana is a special book for them.'

Socialisation of the children is a tough challenge for the couples of inter-religion marriages, since their children are bridges between them and the grandparents. They act as agents of reconciliation. Therefore parents have to be bicultural to ensure that their extended families are part of the larger group and children should not face loss of identity. In one of our case studies, Jasmeet, a Sikh women married to a Muslim narrated that it was very painful for her to see her six-day-old son undergoing circumcision, since this was not part of her earlier culture and also shaving of hair on *Chatti* (six days after birth) was a new cultural experience. Similar considerations have to be addressed by couples when it comes to naming their children, especially when it is the first child, the couple wants a name which echoes their sentiments and also is a reflection of their bicultural attitude. Prof. Mallika named her children Mahak and Chirag, 'it was Muslim and also Hindu. Jasmeet gave her first born an Arabic name so that her in-laws would feel their grandchild had inherited their tradition too. For their second child, she and her husband chose a Persian name. Some couples wanted a "neutral" name, one which would not immediately be identified with the religions they belonged to, and, accordingly, chose a name with a secular meaning. Kamaljeet said, 'when my daughter was born then we decided to have a neutral name. I named her Diya which people of both religions felt comfortable'. One of the respondents of our case studies revealed that she wanted to name her first born Kabir, but her in-laws were somewhat apprehensive, respecting their sentiments she decided to name her son which was acceptable to all. Others didn't want anything "hardcore". Shireen, a Muslim and her Hindu husband Rohit named their daughter Sarah, 'it was Muslim and also Christian.' For Nafisa Begum's mother, the 'relationship with my grandchild is very good. We love him so much. When he was born, we started calling him Gunu and my daughter's mother-in-law gave him the name, Imdad. We have no problem as he is their blood.'

The pattern of religious socialisation of children poses a much greater problem to the inter-religious married couple, especially because the couple has been socialised in different faiths. When the couple belongs to the same religion, there is no difficulty in imparting religious training to the children. The picture, however, changes dramatically when the couple belongs to different religious groups and the burden on the couple seems to be rather heavy when the question for the religious affiliation of children comes up for consideration.

With different religious background married couples are often burdened with difficulties regarding religious affiliation especially in connection with the socialisation of their children. Only when the parents have resolved the possible ambivalence in this regard and have decided on the course of action the problem loses its severity. These difficulties are invariably resolved by the decision: to convert to the faith of the other spouse, so that the child has a uniform religious background and a homogeneously religious home. For Md. Arif, 'children would follow the father's religion. At the time of marriage, my wife has converted so we are both Muslims. Then the children would also follow Islam.'

The difficulties loom large however, in those instances where the choice is still to be made and the parents are still confused regarding the solution. It was observed that half the conflicts between the couples were based on religion, even occurring among those couples, who otherwise professed to be indifferent to their children's religious upbringing. Only in one of our case studies the wife feels that her husband disapproves of the children participating in the festivals of her original faith, but the husband's interview does not bear this out. Riyaz-ud-din said, 'On Holi and Diwali, we go to my in-laws' house after one day. We don't go the same day. We don't take our daughter also. This is because we think that at this age, she will be influenced and it will lead to confusion because we know that when she grows up she will understand everything. Children are very smart now'. This was also the only case where the child's name itself was seen by the mother, as one more religious imposition by the father.

Regarding the choice of their children's religion, on the whole, it was observed that a majority of the children were brought up in their father's faith. For Dr Khalida, 'my two daughters follow Islam because by birth they are Muslim. Our Indian society is a patriarchal society. But they go to the mandir with me also.' Another respondent Aftab expressed similiar sentiments, 'our society is patriarchal. Thus children would follow the father's religion. It depends on the individual's thinking.' A very small number of respondents feel satisfied that they can effectively deal with the problems connected with the child's freedom of choice in the matter of religion. Many, in spite of what they claim, however, find it difficult to allow the child any freedom in the selection of a religion. Indeed, there is almost an implicit assumption on the part of each parent that the child will probably select his faith. And for Rachna Chauhan, 'my children follow Islam. They read the Quran and offer namaz occasionally. But we are giving them an Islamic atmosphere. I am teaching them to respect all religions and treat Hindus and Muslims as the same.' Thus when marriage partners agree to allow their children to select their own religious affiliations, they often feel that the child will select his (the parents) particular religion', Lantz and Synder

(1969: 245). This indicates that, regardless of the intellectual commitments, the appropriate emotional response which is necessary to fulfil these commitments may not be forthcoming.

There is a peculiar dilemma faced by the parents even when the decision regarding the choice of religion is left entirely to the children after they attain a certain age level. What is to be done before it? How should the children be equipped so that they should take this decision freely and yet objectively? This demands strict neutrality—and it is indeed very difficult to take such a stand as the parents have to abandon their own religious commitment. Amir Zaidi says, 'we never taught our children about any religion. I have no knowledge of what religion they are following.' One of the respondent in Abdullahi (2005: 127) says, 'I have no views about my son's religion. I feel I shouldn't interfere in his life. I shouldn't make him a slave of my thinking. Otherwise his potential will be lost. I didn't get my son circumcised though it's good, medically, because it would have been seen as me asserting my religion.'

Quite a few couples, have decided to bring up, their children as belonging to both faiths, and to give the children freedom to decide how to articulate their religious identity. Among some couples, one partner is more religious than the other and is more involved in the religious upbringing. Even then they consciously do not impose their own religion on the child. Between Amrita and Aijaz, Aijaz is more devoutly Muslim, and is also culturally still very much a North Indian Muslim. Aijaz also takes his daughter to see the *Ramlila* (a dramatic folk reenactment of the life of Lord Ram) during the *Dussehra* holidays, one of the main Hindu festivals. Surjana who gave almost identical views regarding her child's upbringing. She said, 'we have decided to expose our daughter to both religions. We are initiating her into both religions. She goes to the temple with me and she also knows namaz. She offers namaz with her father. We won't force anything on her. She will participate with us in whatever we do, and when she grows up, she can decide what she wants. We would be happy if she followed both religions.'

The couples invariably had not left the decision regarding religious affiliation to their children, but had made it themselves. They firmly believed that lack of religious identity would create confusion for children. In spite of this very liberal posture most of these respondents firmly believed that social acceptance of children is facilitated if they are given paternal religious identity, especially as we still use the father's surname and Indian society is patrilineal. After all, adopting the father's religion does simplify matters. 'I never force my children to follow a particular religion but I want them to choose their father's religion because they have to live a long life and if I try to initiate my sons into my religion, it would not be fruitful for their future and I am happy that they have chosen their father's religion. This has happened because I have brought up my children in the Islamic way', said Bhawna Kumari, now Samira.

It is indeed interesting to note that the couples were not in complete harmony about their children's religious socialisation. Goode (1965) has pointed out in this context, that a lot of objection is raised to the religious initiation of children in one faith. Thus, in inter-marriage, children are often the cause of conflict. On the other hand, they are sometimes responsible for the reconciliation of opposing grandparents belonging to either side. Most of the couples had discussed this problem before marriage and again before the birth of a child. Yet their final decision was influenced by the set of parents who showed greater understanding of this problem.

In relation to the rites and rituals, excluding the rites of passage the parents take a moderate and conciliatory view. 'My *Nani* does *puja*. She gives me *parshad* which I eat. For me, it is wheat mixed with sugar. I do not participate in *aarti* (a hindu ritual of worship) and apply *tilak*' (a mark worn on the forehead by Hindus as a religious symbol) says Ishaq Husain's daughter, Ayesha Hasan. She further adds, 'I like Eid most. Then I like Diwali because I see it like our Shabe-e-barat'.

Couples of bicultural marriages do not object to their children observing the rites and rituals of the spouse. At the same time, however, they are not happy about their children adopting their spouse's form of worship and prayer. 'I avoid sending my children to my in-laws for *pujas*, etc. I do send them to watch *Dussehra*. I have to wipe the *tilak* from my forehead before I enter my house so that my mother should not have a cultural shock', says Ishaq Husain. This is undoubtedly contradictory and puzzling. One possible explanation, however, may be that prayer and worship is in a relative sense more personal and intimate; it is in these areas that our respondents appear to be more sensitive. Rites and rituals are more or less external manifestations of social conformity. They, therefore, are guided by norms of social conformity in this area.

Another likely explanation is that, evidently the greater burden of socialisation falls on the female. It is believed that she brings up the child according to her religious pattern and imparts the knowledge she has acquired. After all she belongs to a certain religion and is well conversant with the pattern of worship, prayer, rites and rituals of her faith. The particular aspect of socialisation becomes extraordinarily burdensome, when the mother is expected to instruct the child in the father's religion, about which she herself knows very little. For Bhawna Kumari now Samira, 'I find this new religion good so I am practising it. I can't say anything bad about my previous religion because I have faith in that too.'

Mothers who convert, are quite often unable to proceed with the religious socialisation of the children. Yet they have a great influence on their children compared to the father, as they are in closer proximity till the school-going age. Both the parents agree that the mother's influence on the children is far greater than that of the father. The psychological consequences of the mother's role are important as they give a certain emotional security and create a sense of religious identity in the minds of children. For Pooja now Zeba, 'my children's religious identity is Islam, this is because I have created an

Islamic atmosphere in my home. Maulvi Sahib comes to teach them in Arabic. Currently, my son is studying 25 verse of the Quran.'

As mentioned earlier, religious training quite often is a matter of dispute, specially if both the parents are religious-minded. Often the maternal privilege of child rearing may be challenged by the husband's insistence on up bringing. Observation shows that the mother exerts the greatest influence on the religiosity of the children. In case, both the father and the mother do not wish to instruct or are unable to do so, the grandparents of the child may enter the scene. For Anwari Khanam, it is a moment of pride when her grandchildren recites the *Kalma*. She proudly announces to all her relatives, her grandchildren's belief in Islam and feels proud that her grandchildren are initiated into her culture but then there are cases where daughters-in-laws are not happy with this kind of interference regarding the religious orientation of their children. There is one case where the wife speaks of the mother-in-law's indoctrination of the child into the religion of the husband's family, although the husband himself is not religious, and she is unable to resist the pressure. Women especially have to negotiate the religious pressure excerted by the families. The grand parents both maternal and paternal want their grandchildren to adopt the religious practices of their faith.

A greater number of children in this study were instructed in the religious sphere by their father's parents. A considerable number were instructed by other agencies such as the school and religious classes, while only a few were given religious instructions by their own father. Two interviewees in Chopra and Punwani (2005: 128) mention that they expect some "push-and-pull" or "give-and take" regarding the grandparents' approach to children's identity. In a case, the wife (who has converted to Islam) feels her parents will insist that her children visit the temple, which neither she nor her husband want. She says she will have to figure out a 'nice way' to tell them but 'it will be difficult.' In another case, the wife, herself a child of mixed parentage, feels disconcerted at the prospect of the in-laws insisting on the child following their customs and faith, but also consoles herself with the thought that there will be "cross-ventilation" by her family as well as by the couple themselves. There are couples who very briefly mention one set of parents being unhappy with the name given to a child, either because it is clearly identifiable with one religion, or because it is not identifiable with either.

In our study, there were many cases where relations with the grandchildren of the parents of the couple are good. For Aijaz's mother, Munni Begum, 'when my son comes here he comes with his daughter and we love her. We think that she did not do anything then why should we take revenge on a small girl. She is my granddaughter so we love her.' For another respondent, Amit Arora, 'the relationship with my grandchildren is good. Just because what my daughter did I can't punish my grandchildren. How is it their fault? They are very close to us.'

Grandparents meet the children of the couple after they have accepted the marriage, for Rachna Chauhan, 'now my parents have reconciled. They meet me and give gifts to my children. Thus my children like their Nana-Nani (maternal grand parents) very much.'

One can know how precious the grandchild can be as stated by the father of Md. Alam, Mushtaq Khan, 'we used to say that the grandchild is more important than the son. I have only one granddaughter and she is our life. We can't live without her. We love her so much that sometimes we are apprehensive that we are spoiling her. We are so attached to her that we cannot express it. It can only be perceived.' For the mother of Md. Alam, Imrana Ara, 'our relationship with my granddaughter is good. She is everyone's darling, both paternal and maternal grandparents love her.'

There is the case where the maternal grandfather of the child does not love the child but the rest of the family loves the child. For Sanjana now Zoya, 'my father does not talk to my daughter, he does not care for her. But he observes her and remembers my childhood. My mother and Bhabi love my daughter'. On the other hand Sanjana's mother-in-law, said, 'I have many grandchildren but I love her more than I love my other grandchildren.'

Children of mixed marriages go through different cultural experiences. Their bicultural upbringing and their attitude to society specifically to kinship relationships is based on their experiences. In one case a grandchild was not liked because of the difference of religion between the grandparents and the grandchild. For Sanya daughter of Amin, 'in my paternal family, we children are accepted and loved but in my maternal family we did not get appreciation and affection. This is because their feeling was that we are Muslim and we practise Islamic rituals, which was not acceptable.' In another case the grandmother doesn't liked the grandchild because of the religious difference. Arifa Husain's comment about her mother, Meena, 'she does not love and is not so close to my daughter. She thinks that my daughter is Muslim as she follows Islam.' And last but not the least, for daughter of Koyal Sharma now Nagma Alam, 'my *Nani* and *Nana* both love me very much. I go every Sunday and come back at night.' They never treat me harshly.' By and large, the grandchildren were loved by their grandparents even if the parents of the grandchildren had an inter-religion marriage.

All told, the couples that have children or spoke of children's identities, there is general agreement between the couples about the upbringing of the child. As mentioned in the earlier section, in-laws generally respect the space of the couple. It is difficult to form any generalisations whether the line between personal and familiar space gets more blurred and complicated in the case of children, the majority do not bring up the topic of in-laws or grandparents staking a claim to the identity of the child or teaching them about religion.

Often, the identity of children appears to be understood in two broad ways, although the boundaries between the two are often extremely fuzzy, and there is tension between two understandings. On the one hand, the identity of their children is understood as formed by both faiths, and it is emphasised that the child's religious identity cannot be viewed as only Hindu or only Muslim. For Muslim Khan, 'I am giving my daughter a secular atmosphere. I have no problem when she goes to the mandir with her Nani. When she goes to her *Dadi*'s (paternal grandmother) place, she sees that during Azan everyone covers their heads. She also follows that.' On the other hand, in interviewees' narratives it was often assumed, taken for granted, or clarified that the children are officially or de facto of one faith, usually the father's religion. For example, Preeti says, 'My sons are Muslims—that's the religion we have put down in their school certificates.' But these couples are categorical that their children will be free to follow whatever faith they wish when they grow up.

Chopra and Punwani (2005) discuss that the decision to orient, officially or otherwise, the children more towards one faith is often a pragmatic choice to minimise societal opposition and the problems children might face. It is also motivated by the knowledge that in official documents such as school forms or passports, there is no mechanism that recognises or acknowledges an inter-religious identity. Indeed, parents are highly conscious that Indian society views an individual as belonging to either one or another religion but not to both. Hence, even where their instincts revolt against making the choice for their children, they force themselves to do so.

At the same time, parents are equally committed to emphasising the dual religious heritage of their children, a no less agonising choice. One of the respondent in Chopra and Punwani reveals that when her daughter had to fill a form, she refused to write her religion. She told her teacher that her mother and father had different religions, and finally wrote "none of the above". Two other respondents in their study have stuck to their guns whenever they have had to fill in the religion of their child in official forms, however difficult it may have been. One describes her daughter's religion as 'humanism'. While other always leaves the space blank.

Children as a symbol and marker of an inter-religion marriage often provoke hostility in social spaces, especially when their identity as such is made apparent. Couples report teachers and school officials singling out their children and confronting the latter with questions about their identity. Pooja narrates , 'once we took our children to my hometown to Gorakhpur (in the state of Uttar Pradesh) during the Diwali holidays. They were thrilled because they got to celebrate the Diwali holidays with their maternal cousins. Since I have three brothers, so they got to celebrate Diwali thrice in three different homes of my relatives. This meant a lot of crackers, gifts and merry making. The next day when they mentioned this to their tutor, he said, "what do you have to do with Diwali?" The coaching would continue during the Diwali vacation. They felt very hurt and told their mother about this. Sometimes classmates, friends, acquaitances and neighbours are also the agents of discrimination and hostility against children.

At times these children are exposed to pestering questions by their friends and other children about their religious identity. Even small children had to face tough questions especially from neighbourhood friends. 'Are you a Hindu or a Muslim or neither? In one of the cases, an inter-religious married couple, who was a Hindu married to a Muslim and living in a Muslim-dominated area once faced a very interesting question by her son. One day her son who was 5 years old at the time asked her- 'who is a *kafir* (non-believer)?' She said, 'why are you asking this question?' He said; 'my friends are calling me a "kafir", is it an abuse?' His mother explained to him that there is only one God and He has created the universe. Anyone who believes in God is a believer and not a "kafir".' Even a 5-year-old child is not spared by the neighbours who make him conscious of the fact that he is 'different' from them because his mother and father belong to two different religious communities. This little boy was able to reconcile the two religions in a beautiful manner which the parents often quoted to their friends. He would say *'Allah-miyan ki Jai'*. *Allah Miyan* is a typical expression used by the

Muslim community to refer to God and *Jai* is a typical Hindu expression in praise of God.

Hamid and Preeti's son was asked by one of his classmates why he lives in India? He should go to Pakistan. Such experiences leave a deep impression on the minds of growing children and it is also painful experience for the parents, especially mothers. Many Hindu women married to Muslim men in our case study expressed this fear and concern in regard to the security of their husbands and children. 'I feel threatened whenever there are incidences of violence between the two communities, I do not allow my husband and son to go out'. At times I have to bear the comments of my relatives who say that *'tum tuo marney walono sey peetney wallano mey chali gai'* (you have shifted from the community of beaters to beaten).

The impact of inter-religion marriages on children is perhaps the most important part of the study. Such inter-religion marriages bring about changes in the lives of the couple, their parents and particularly the children. It was, therefore, very crucial to interview the children. Unfortunately, however, children consisted of the smallest section of the sample because the majority of the children of the couples interviewed were too young to respond. Also many parents did not want the researcher to reveal to their young children that their parents had an inter-religious marriage. Thus, only children who were grown up and aware of their parents' bicultural marriage could be interviewed and not all of them were willing to talk about the inter-religious marriages of their parents and its impact on their lives. Children who were well adjusted and enjoyed the support of both the families —i.e. mother's and father's family were more forthcoming and willing to talk about their experiences of their parents' inter-religion marriages. Children, who had suffered social boycott or humiliation because of their parents were less forthcoming and some even refused to be interviewed on the subject.

The experiences of the children from mixed marriages are insightful and innocent reflections. For Iqbal, son of Amjad and Bhawana, 'when I was 6 year-old, I came to know that my parents had an inter-religion marriage. Neither did my Dadi say anything against my mother nor did my Nani say anything against my father. I don't feel any confusion at all. I feel happy when my mother offers namaz.'

The school also plays a very important role in the lives of the children of inter-religion marriages. If the school provides a secular environment, the children learn secular values and respect the decision of their parents to get married in spite of belonging to different religions. But schools which promote fundamentalist ideologies make the adjustments of children of such inter-religious marriages more difficult. In the case of the child being mentioned above, he was sent to a school which was known for its secular ideology and one day one of the boy's classmates teased him for having parents of two different religious communities. The boy reported the matter to the teacher concerned. The teacher immediately gave a strong lecture in the class on secular values and how secularism is essential for making a person a good human being. That had a very deep impact on the child as well as on all the other children in the class. It contributed not only to his adjustment to the inter-religion marriage of his parents but he also developed a sense of pride in the secular values he got from his parents who belonged to two different religious communities.

Some children, for example, were proud of their parents decisions to have gone for inter-religion marriage. For Dr Sheikh's son, 'I am proud of my parents' marriage. I think that what they did, especially my mother, was courageous.' There were others who were happy with their decision to get married, but felt they did not have enough family support and support of the society because of which adjustments had been very difficult. Life had been very difficult for such couples. And, they hoped that their children would not face such problems when they grew up and wanted to get married. They hoped that the society would gradually become more secular and accept and support such marriages especially when it is time for their (inter-religion) couples' children to get married.

Grown up adults and children whose parents had been married for more than 15-20 years, knew that their parents had inter-religion marriages. The reactions of children to such marriages varied extremely from very positive to very negative depending on the socio-economic, educational background of the parents and the locality/ñeighbourhood in which they lived and their own life experiences. Each case, in a way, was unique and exclusive. Reactions of children of inter-religion marriages depended on the conditions, circumstances, educational background, neighbourhood, family background, friendship-groups, upbringing, experience of the partition of the country, personal relationships between Hindus and Muslims and in many cases political affiliations of the family and the couples. The overall adjustment of the couples to the family and to the society and their reactions to inter-religion marriages were influenced by all the above mentioned factors and all these in turn had a deep impact on the lives and reactions of the children to the inter-religion marriage of their parents. But when such a family lives in a mixed neighbourhood where most religious communities, cultures, and traditions are represented, the children also learn to adapt themselves to a multicultural lifestyle. Their adjustment to the inter-religion marriage of their parents is facilitated by the multicultural ethos of the neighbourhood. Malika lived in a Muslim-dominated area. Her son, around five or six years old, was finding it difficult to adjust to the inter-religion marriage of his parents because of the embarrassing questions being posed to him by his friends in the neighbourhood. He was even teased by them and he found it difficult to cope with the situation. But as soon, as the family moved to a more cosmopolitan area, his adjustment to his parents' inter-religion marriage became easier and he started enjoying the dual cultures of his parents and became very popular with his friends in the neighbourhood and in his school.

When the parents married for love and cut across religious barriers, it is important to know how liberal they are with their children in the matter of choice of friends and free mixing with the other sex which may lead to choice of the mate.

It was an interesting observation that we got different reactions to this issue. 'I can't impose anything on my daughter. Even in her marriage, if it is inter-religion then how can I prevent her? I will support her', Zahid husband of Kamaljeet. She adds, 'I will teach my children to respect all religions, to be good human beings and never fight for religion. I will not force my children to marry into my religion or my husband's religion. I have chosen my partner myself. Therefore they would have the right to choose their partners themselves'. Sanya, daughter of Ambika and Amir was brought up in a completely liberal atmosphere. She says, 'I would prefer to marry a Muslim because I think I am a religious person. Thus it is good for me to choose a partner who belongs to a Muslim family. I could marry a Hindu also but I know that I cannot make the necessary adjustments.'

The question of mate selection and marriage of the children assumes greater significance due to the inter-religion marriage of parents. Most of the parents wanted to help and guide their children in the right direction. Though the respondents had made their choice entirely on their own, they invariably expressed the opinion that after all marriage is a very serious matter and it should not be left entirely to the children. 'What my children intend to do, I hope they will inform us. We would give them freedom for choosing their partner but they should tell us their choice. This is because we hurt our parents. Thus I don't want my children to do the same', Sanjana Rawat, now Zoya Khan.

Sarita Agnihotri now Sakina Khanam, 'I prefer that my children should choose partners who are educated and open minded. Their family should be good. It is not necessary that one has to be a Muslim. The person whom my children are going to marry, should be good human beings.' This is a traditional value expressed by the couples. Here, the experience of one couple is worth relating. The female was a Muslim and the male was a Hindu. They had retained their religious identity. When their daughters grew up, the parents gave them complete liberty in the choice of life partners. 'One of my daughters got married to a Hindu. It was a civil marriage. He did not convert and neither was it important for my daughter. But for me conversion was important because I am a religious person', said Razia. 'I will support their choice for a life partner. Even if he is a Hindu I have no problem. Both my parents and my in-laws participated in our marriage. Nobody created any problem', said Ruchi Arif.

Children of such marriages who were brought up in a secular environment learnt to respect all religions. They also tend to choose life partners irrespective of the religious ideology of the other person. In a family where a couple had an inter-religion marriage, nearly forty years ago, the daughter got married to a Muslim and the son got married to a Hindu. This was considered to be a natural thing to have happened. The parents of these children took pride in the fact that their children had grown-up to be such secular-minded responsible individuals who could choose their life partners without religion being a consideration. This is a true example of secular upbringing of children in a family which has experienced inter-religion marriage. In another case where a Muslim girl had married a Hindu boy, the son got married to a Hindu girl, but there is so much respect for Islam in the family that it was difficult for a stranger to make out whether it was a Hindu or Muslim family.

They are more open to the probability of selecting the mate from the other community since the other community is not strictly "other" for them, which further results in communal harmony.

Children of inter-faith marriages become religious "hybrids" in which they blend the religious perspectives of both the parents. Their socialisation, thus leads to bicultural exposure. They also face rejections from their extended families and face identity conflicts. They in turn become more tolerant and harmonious than their counterpart offspring of homogamous marriages. Thus, a mixed marriage is a process of social change. The traits, attitudes and behaviour of mixed heritage children are exposed to bicultural socialisation, which in turn leads to tolerance and harmonious living in the society. Park (1950) commented that exposure to multiple cultures causes the marginal person to become 'the individual with the wide horizon, the keener intelligence, the more rational and detected viewpoint... the most civilised of human creatures.' Thus, children raised in mixed heritage homes would be less prejudiced, dogmatic and xenophobic, as well as more cognitively flexible and emphatic.

The children of inter-religious marriage couples can be the agents of positive social change in this communally divided society. Since they inherit the legacies of two different religions from their parents, even if they follow any one religion, mostly their father's, they have relatives of both religions. The kin groups belonging to two different religions are the source of their primary socialisation which makes them emotionally attached to families of grandparents of both sides. This primary socialisation, later on in life, inhibits the development of prejudices against the other community. These children become a very cohesive group which helps in binding the society.

6

Challenges to Inter-Religion Marriages

In India kinship ties are very strong and a large number of people continue to live in joint families. Marriage is not a bond between just husband and wife but a bond between families. In inter-religion marriages most families oppose the decision of the young couples to get married. The level of resistance may vary from mild to very severe but most families oppose such marriages for various reasons. When an individual intends to choose a partner of a different religion, he or she is already prepared for a conflict situation. The hornet's nest that may be aroused, could make them cautious. Pre-marital difficulties start surfacing at the beginning only. The period of courting is very long and the couple tries to make all possible efforts to win over the support of their parents as the consent is very important. Though the institution of family and marriage is going through tremendous change in Indian society, the consent of parents is still valued.

Therefore, the couples take a much longer period to get married when it comes to inter-religion marriage. It was generally observed that there was a substantial time gap between the first meeting of the couple, liking for each other, decision to get married, getting married and announcement of the marriage. Considering that Hindu-Muslim marriages are the most difficult inter-religion marriages in India, the time frame is much more flexible.

In modern society, individualism is preferred over

collectivity. Not only have the patterns of mate selection itself undergone drastic change, increased exposure to women gives them more opportunities to intermingle at educational and economic institutions. Love marriages are quite common. But in case of inter-caste and inter-religion marriages we find societal reaction opposing such alliances. During their initial contact, the companions find that there is an irresistible attraction between them—a common academic background, a comparable economic status, certain common interests and beliefs, or practices pertaining to different spheres of life, physical beauty, etc. This powerful mutual attraction gave the couple the necessary impetus to meet repeatedly, enabling them to understand each other as thoroughly as possible.

Apart from the cases where occupational and residential proximity helped them to meet almost every day, special efforts were made by the spouses to meet very often and discuss matters of mutual interest. Such frequent meetings enable them to realise the problems that would arise out of an inter-marriage. For Babita Arora, now Farhana Afreen, wife of Shakir Afreen, 'I met my husband in a business association and we were friends for four years. Then we decided to get married.' Naturally the meetings were invariably clandestine till the time of marriage. The respondents' courting phase ranged from approximately a year to more than eight years, and in one case, it was ten years. Therefore, the most commonest pattern amongst these love-lorn couples was to 'carry on courtship. For Payal, wife of Zubain 'we both knew each other from childhood. And decided to get married.' Zubain said, 'I could not think of somebody else, we had to wait a long time.'

Women are never free from their social and moral obligations. There were many respondents who were first generation learners, their family backgrounds were liberal, they were motivated by their parents to study and make their careers. While studying they met their prospective husbands. Here again the conditioning of women who were considered to be obedient, to be loyal to their family, made them take the decision to be loyal to their husbands. Almost all the cultures teach women that her husband is her God. So this socialisation along with the fear of being in a relationship with the man of the opposite community compelled women to strongly stick to their boyfriends. 'Since my childhood my mother has been telling me that commitment is the integral part of a successful marriage. How can I cheat somebody? I cannot be loyal to anyone except him'. Here the concern of the respondent as in patriarchy is she is not going to win the trust and dignity of any man for her premarital affair, 'I had no option. I had to disobey my parents.' For Manjari now Noor, 'my parents came to know about my marriage after I got married. So they could not prevent it, but lodged a police complaint against my husband. They tried their best to convince me. We really had a tough time escaping. They were putting a lot of emotional pressure on me to break the marriage'. Also once the decision is taken, marriage itself gets postponed for various reasons, specially because of the fear of reaction or non-acceptance by their own families.

In India, since caste and religion are basic criteria in the selection of a mate in the kin-oriented choice, self-choice and love-matches are looked upon with complete disapproval. Besides that, parental objection becomes more severe with the pressure from the religious group. Another important factor used to dissuade couples from such marriages was that it becomes very difficult for the younger siblings of both girls and boys, and more so in the case of girls to get married if the older brother or sister has had an inter-religion marriage.

'There was a lot of pressure on my husband from his natal family to get married as his parents were aware that he was having an affair with a non-Muslim girl and they were against this idea. They did not want him to marry. Therefore they made him go back often to his native place on one pretext or other. It became difficult for him to deal with the family pressure. Therefore we married in 1993, but being the eldest child in the family, I did not disclose this to my family as I had two younger siblings to get married', said Jasmeet. Acceptance of such marriages by the wider society is not easy although such marriages generally take place within the higher socio-economic levels with a relatively high education background. Yet endogamous marriages enjoy social approval, whereas such marriages have to face discrimination from the society.

After deciding to get married most couples tried to persuade their parents and siblings to grant them permission to get married. The process often took a lot of time and persuasion. Some couples were fortunate enough to get the support of their parents and here too, the girl's parents took much longer to accept the marriage or even with the decision of their daughter to get married, some of them did not accept the marriage at all.

The reasons for the opposition by the parents of our respondents in all phases beginning from courting to the final performance of the marriage ceremony are many. Since the boy and girl belong to different religions, not only do they not have the approval of the parents but, often have a strong reaction from the families, relatives, friends of the two communities involved. Hindus/Sikhs and Muslims are seen as opposite to each other in terms of culture, traditions, religion, food habits and also politically they are seen as majority versus minority. Thus falling in love with a person of the "opposite" religion or culture may be easy but the decision to get married is the most difficult one and getting the approval of the parents even more difficult. Everybody dissuades the couple from getting married. For Babita Arora now Farhana Afreen, 'I think such a marriages should happen. This is because there is a misconception about Islam. Other people have no knowledge about Islam. Earlier I thought that Muslims are bad, they eat meat and they marry more than once, which is not true. Thus such marriages should happen, to bring the two communities together and remove all the stereotypes which people of both communities have about each other.'

Socially after the marriage, the couple generally face's boycott. They are isolated and often not invited by their families, relatives and friends for any rituals, festivals, functions, etc. At times this opposition becomes so strong that in one case the parents had completely disowned the daughter and she was not invited to any weddings or festivals. The worst happened when she was not even informed about the death of her father. Furthermore, in many cases the couple loses the sense of belonging and develops a kind of insecurity. Marriages which are not arranged by parents are usually not always supported by the siblings and close relatives.

The parents of the couple also face the problem of isolation from their religious community. They are generally held responsible for breaking the norms set up by the religion. In addition to this they carry the guilt feeling as they get caught in the conflict of loyalty between their community and their children. For Preeti, 'I am sure that they would not be happy with my inter-religious marriage. Even after seven years whenever my neighbours inquire about my whereabouts from my mother she has no answer. My mother calls me and asks, 'tell me what should I tell them? They cannot stop gossiping and complaining. I do not think that there will be an improvement in their thinking over the years.'

The fact is that all inter-religious marriages are love marriages or self-arranged marriages and generally do not have the approval of the parents and the society as opposed to marriages arranged by parents within the caste and within the religious community. The degree of disapproval may vary from one case to the other and may be minimal in celebrity marriages. In such cases the celebrity status of one or both partners overrides religious differences of the partners.

In arranged marriages the families and close relatives are a great source of support and provide stability to arranged marriages. But that is not the case in inter-religion marriages such couples are almost totally deprived of family support. Furthermore, important questions need to be addressed by the couple before they get married. These are the questions posed by parents, relatives, siblings and friends. What will be the future of their children? Will the society accept them? What will be the death rituals for them? Will it be a cremation, burial, electric cremation or organ donation?

Parents, relatives and friends scare the couple and especially the girl if she is marrying a Muslim, they tell her things like, 'Talaq is so easy amongst the Muslims. What is the guarantee that you will not be divorced?' Furthermore, since polygamy is permitted to Muslims and religion permits them to marry up to four wives; 'do you want to be one of the four wives?'

Another important question that is posed is a legal question. Legally on conversion, one loses one's inheritance rights in parental property. Whether you are a Hindu or a Muslim, you lose your inheritance rights after conversion. Many couples did report that they had not claimed their share in ancestral property due their inter-religion marriages, the actual reason quoted by the majority of couples was that they wanted to live life on their own terms and conditions. For Surjana, wife of Farahatullah, 'property matters have not come up so far. But in Hindu families the daughter does not get anything. So there is no question of property. On my husband's side, property is undivided. Both of us don't think about these things.' Loss of inheritance is used as bargaining power to dissuade couples from getting married.

Also conversion is generally not favoured by society. One acquires religion at birth. In one case conversion became an issue and came in the way of a Hindu-Muslim marriage. We came across a Hindu boy and a Muslim girl who were having a love affair for many years. When they decided to get married, the parents of the girl insisted that the boy should convert to Islam. But he refused and the marriage did not take place.

'You cannot change religion at birth and if it is meant to be used as an easy way to get married there is even greater opposition.' Sometimes, such couples are even treated as outcastes, alienated and disowned by society, except if they belong to the elite class.

Family friends, relatives and, everybody else demotivates the couple who decides to get married that such marriages are very taxing, emotionally and socially. Couples described the societal opposition they have faced because of being in an inter-religion marriage. The Muslim interviewees as well as those who had converted to Islam for marriage reported encountering prejudicial remarks or attitudes from their spouse's relatives. After the marriage negative remarks from in-laws are even more pronounced than at the point of time they learnt of their son or daughter's intention to marry a Muslim. Usually after the marriage, even where in-laws have grudgingly or gradually accepted the marriage, there is cordiality and civility in interaction. After marriage, remarks of a communal nature from in-laws tend to be occasional. Jasmeet comments about her father, 'he thinks that Muslims can marry more than one wife. They divorce easily. Even though his impression about Muslims has now improved, he is not prepared to accept this.' It should also be noted that some parents have cut off their relations, or maintain very limited relations with their son or daughter after the inter-religion marriage. In these cases, while parents may continue to hold strongly negative views about their son-in-law's or daughter-in-law's faith, the scope for expressing such sentiments is limited. After the marriage, mostly a sibling, cousin, or another member of the extended family are the chief perpetrators of prejudicial comments and attitudes. The following examples reflect interviewees' experiences in this regard. For Jyoti now Nargis, 'my parents had many problems that in a Muslim family, men did two or three marriages they are not educated, they do not practice family planning and live in unhealthy ghettos. My parents failed to realise that muslims lived in secluded localities not for security but they are not welcome in mixed residential localities.

It took Renuka ten years to get the consent of her mother to marry Nasim. Her family's opposition to her marrying a Muslim was very strong. Even after her marriage they have regrets that they allowed her, to marry a Muslim 'They are still prejudiced about Muslims, 'they criticise their polygamous attitude and comment' they have four wives, they beat their wives.' In another case, Arjuman earlier Shashikala's father still refuses to speak to her. Though the mother and sisters visited her where she lived with her husband, despite the fact that they did not like the Muslim colony, Zakir Nagar, Okhla in which she now lives. 'They keep asking me to move out of that locality.' She is often taunted that she is living among dirty people, who have no sense of hygiene and cleanliness. They also want her to look "modern" and stop wearing salwar kurtas. I often argue with my mother why she does not have the same objection for her sister when she complies with the traditions and culture of her in-laws.

Samira feels that Indian society as a whole is anti-Muslim. She says that her friends and relatives keep giving adverse comments on Muslims. They were burdened with the stereotypical concept of Muslims of being violent, rigid, orthodox and polygamists. The politicisation of religion has led to communalisation of Indian society. This phenomena has effected the couples in inter-religion marriages. Particularly woman from Hindu community are more vulnerable.

Three couples experienced the threat of violence acutely post Babri Mosque demolition riots (1992-93). Alka and Sageer had applied for court marriage at Tees Hazari Court. Alka's house was in a West Delhi locality and they were attacked twice by an RSS-led mob. She heard them shout, asking her father to keep her under his control otherwise he would face serious consequences. Her father had a heart attack. He was hospitalised. Alka had already done nikah and legally she was the wife of Sageer. Sageer had to flee to escape the wrath of Hindu communalists. Alka's family was also threatened. Though she went back briefly, she could not bear to stay on there. She shifted for a while to a relative's home in Mumbai. Alka and Sageer were thinking of migrating to Canada after a court marriage, this plan has become a compulsion. 'The communalist forces like VHP. RSS doesn't want Hindu-Muslim unity, so we'll have to go, ' says Alka simply. She says, 'The RSS won't let us be together. I have converted, but we want to have both kinds of marriages. And let our children imbibe the best of both religions.'

One sphere of activity where couples faced discrimination was of residence. In Western society it is an accepted norm that a couple sets up an independent home after marriage. But in India, due to the sentiments of the traditional joint family system, the son invariably brings his bride to his parental home. In mixed marriages the daughter-in-law, therefore, is sometimes an unwelcome member to the household. Couples were forced to look for an independent or neo-local residence, since there is lack of support for such marriages. Life became difficult, and more so in a communally charged atmosphere such a marriage becomes a source of alienation. The societal opposition increases many fold.

For an inter-religion married couple, purchasing a house or renting an apartment, if it was in a non-Muslim area was not easy. For example, Kusum Verma could not move into the flat she and her husband bought, because "no one would give it to a Muslim." Couples also reported discrimination or at the very least, curiosity, from neighbours and acquaintances, in subtle and not-so subtle forms when people came to know one of the partners is Muslim. Many couples who were looking for rented accommodation in predominantly Hindu-dominated areas reported that the landlords refused on the pretext of not renting their house to "non-vegetarians", instead of openly refusing it to such a couple. One respondent informed that the couple tried to get accommodation in a society and were on the verge of shifting there when the residents of that area became aware of their inter-religion marriage and objected to their staying as they feared it could be bad example for their children. So then they had no other option left, but to shift to a Muslim-dominated area of South Delhi.

Another respondent, Rizwana Khatoon married to a Hindu husband, Naresh reported that she accepted Hindu symbols of marriage like *sindoor* and *mangalsutra*. She would limit her socialisation with neighbours and would meet them during festivals. She accepted *Prashad* to avoid suspicions of being Muslim. Still, she and her husband would be ridiculed occasionally which would often upset her. As she says, all this made her want to move out and they have since moved into a more mixed colony.

Amir and Suman are a modern couple residing in a multicultural housing society. 'Nobody knew at first that Amir was a Muslim. One day when his grandfather came from the village to live with us, people found out that he was Muslim. They turned quite cold.' Recalls Suman, so they would pass remarks such as, 'why have you put on these Muslim songs?', whenever I played a ghazal cassette, they will comment and say that I love ghazals because I am married to muslim. Once I painted my doors in green. They remarked that I am found of green colour because it is muslim colour.

Arti now Amina's isolation is perhaps the most extreme. The isolation is compounded by the fact that she lives with her 'typically Muslim' father-in-law in a lower-middle class Muslim locality in Delhi. She says, 'I had never thought my best friend would change, though she did support me in my marriage, she came to our house recently. She's a Jain, and I felt awful that she did not touch anything we offered her expect fruit and water. But I can understand. I too wouldn't have done so in earlier times, when I was a teenager. I too, used to think that Muslims are dirty.'

Societal opposition encountered in the everyday or routine experiences of living life as an inter-religion couple is, in a sense, different from the violence and threat to life and property experienced at the time of riots. But as mentioned earlier a Hindu-Muslim marriage itself sometimes becomes a provocation for violence, and even where it doesn't, the kind of hostility it arouses is itself a threat to the fundamental right to lead one's life peacefully. The routine discrimination must be placed in the context of the increasing communalisation of Indian life and polarisation between communities. Such communalisation and polarisation, needless to say, is significantly accelerated and exacerbated with the incidence of riots. After the Hindu-Muslim riots of 1992-93, communalisation at the workplace, school or other social spaces in general has increased. The 1992-93 riots and (to a lesser extent) the 2002 Gujarat riots directly affected numerous interviewees, their families, and children.

One couple acutely experienced the threat of violence. Mohammad Ali married to Radhika from Baroda was visiting his in laws at Baroda soon, after the 2002 Gujarat riots. The house where he stayed was attacked twice by an RSS-led mob, after the post-Godhra violence. His wife heard them shout, *Mohammad Ali ko baahar nikalao,* (bring Mohammad Ali out) as she fled to a Hindu neighbour's home. His Hindu (now converted) wife's family was also threatened. They could not bear to stay on in Baroda and came back to Delhi.

It needs to be mentioned that not all couples faced discrimination as a result of being in an inter-religion marriage. Also, several of the interviewees categorically mentioned that they have faced no problems being married to someone from another faith. Yet it should be pointed out that some (though not all) of these very interviewees also narrated particular incidents of discrimination. Arguably, these interviewees do not consider such isolated incidents as typifying ongoing societal opposition. Societal opposition and discrimination is most pronounced in the case of Muslims and those married to Muslims. It also seems to be more acute in the case of women generally, and women married to Muslims in particular. This is possibly explained by the fact that, regardless of whether the woman has converted or not, a woman marrying into another religion is perceived as having gone over to another faith. In contrast, the same is not assumed of men marrying into another religion, unless they have categorically converted and display visible markers of their new faith.

Interviewees reported disparaging comments from government and public officials. Preeti remembers an incident when she went to a reputed hospital, while she was at the registration counter, receptionist asked her about the name of her husband. As Preeti responded the receptionist, commented angrily in Punjabi, *Hore Koyi Nai Millya si* (you did not find anybody else). In another case a close friend who was against his friend(Muslim) marrying a Sikh girl, informed the police that a boy and a girl have eloped and are hiding in a hotel. Though this action of this particular friend led to a strong reaction from their friends and colleagues since all of them were taken to the police 'station and threatened, I have seen the officials' face change colours immediately on reading my name. Similar sentiments are narrated by one of the repspondents in Abdullahi (2005: 57). Once an airport official asked me *'in mein Kya dekha aapne?* (What did you see in him?). That makes me furious and angry. At times I react but at times

I have to tolerate such remarks if I am accompanied by my children.'

Many couples narrated their experiences of discrimination experienced at work place. Rehman, a social activist-and researcher, describes how his being married to a Hindu drew objections from other Muslims in his own organisation. One reason why he faced strong opposition was because his wife Niki wears a bindi and observes the *Karva Chauth* fast (Hindu ritual when a married woman fasts for the long life of her husband).

Several interviewees did categorically state that having a Hindu or Muslim spouse did not create any problem for them during the communal violence. One spoke of the psychological impact, fear of violence, some experience of life being disrupted during riots, or anxiety about safety, if riots were to break out again. A few also emphasised that they did not feel insecure as a Hindu-Muslim couple but they are scared of the communalisation of society. After the Hindu-Muslim riots of 1992-93 and 2002 Gujarat riots, religious discrimination at the workplace, school or other social spaces in general has increased. These riots directly and indirectly affected numerous interviewees, their families, and children. The general atmosphere in society has increased the level of communalisation. In fact after 2002. Godhra riots Indian society has undergone second partition, it has partioned the minds of people. The society is polarised in Hindus and Muslims. 1947 was partition of territories only. For Akbar, the experience shook his faith in his social ideals, he felt betrayed by his friends for not helping enough. He says, 'for me it was as if my friends were standing out there, seeing me in danger and not helping. Now I realise they couldn't have helped.'

Many couples agreed that there was no point living in fear or anxiety others drew attention to the fact that they would not conceal their identities as Muslims or partners in a marriage with a Muslim. They did mention experiences such as having to relocate themselves during the time or the possibility of being affected by violence.

Alka, a Hindu married to a Muslim says the only thing that worries her is 'what if riots break out again, as they had in 1992-93. My husband and his family will suffer because of me.' After the 2002 riots, her parents are apprehensive. She says, 'They've told me, if anything happens, let people think you are Hindu. But I am very clear that if anybody asks me, I shall say who I am.' Preeti, who converted to Islam after marrying Muslim, feels among other reasons, safety is one reason why one partner in such marriages converts. After September 11, her mother was scared for her as she now lives in a predominantly Muslim area, and asked her to come home to her parents' Hindu locality, saying 'they'll kill you'. They won't trust you.' Alka confesses that sometimes she does worry along those lines. She has converted to Islam after marrying Sageer and feels secure in the Muslim area where she now lives, but has started feeling unsafe in some other areas in the city. She remembers an incident at the time of her court marriage and the furore created by BJP/VHP volunteers at her natal home, 'when Godhra was on, I was so terrified.' Preeti worries about her son being targeted. Given the communal climate of the times, she worries, when bomb blast happened in Delhi followed by Batla House encounter I was too scared for the security of my family.'

The children of such couples face very difficult problems and at times, there is no one to fall back on because there is no support system for such couples. The school also plays a very important role in the lives of the children of inter-religion marriages. As mentioned earlier if the school provides a secular environment, the children would learn secular values and respect the decision of their parents to get married in spite of belonging to different religions. But schools which promote fundamentalist ideologies make the adjustments of children of such inter-religious marriages more difficult. The riots also affected children strongly, especially children who were in their formative years. Preeti, whose husband is a Muslim says, 'my children at times are confronted with odd situations. The other day my son was telling me that after the Batla House incident, he felt his standing among his schoolmates had suddenly gone down. He is 12 years old.' Her son didn't feel he was under threat, but he was neither here nor there and has become more conscious of being a Muslim. For both her sons, she says, 'being half-Hindu and half-Muslim, and living through the communal atmosphere definitely created an identity problem.' I feel even more scared because my son is of mixed parentage. If he had been a only Muslim, then at least Muslims would have defended him—if, god forbid, such a situation ever arose. The security of their children is prime concern in the minds of parents of mixed marriages. The bicaltural identity of offsprings at times can make them valurable in communally charged situation like riot etc.

At times it was shared by our respondents that it was difficult to find a suitable match for the children of such mixed marriages because of this dual identity more so for girls than for the boys. As we have seen in the case studies, there were quite a few children even boys of the inter-religious couples who could not get married. It creates a sense of 'double loss of identity' as in one of the cases of inter religion married couple's family. They had a dual identity or loss of identity when they were still young and after the divorce of their parents and change of their names it was a case of almost a second loss of identity for them. These boys did not easily mix with everybody, they had both moved away from home and desperately wanted to marry but could not find suitable matches. They both wanted to get married to Hindu girls because they, along with their mother, were now part of the Hindu fold. As mentioned earlier, they also had Hindu names and their father's name had been dropped from their names after their parents' divorce.

Not only that most families oppose inter-religion marriages but also try their best to prevent it. In such cases, therefore, the bride giving family and the bride receiving family have very little interaction with each other and they almost view each other as 'enemies'. The question of family support for the couple therefore does not arise. This is a major concern for the girl and boy when considering marriage into another religious community. The girl and boy love their families and expect the same from them. But when they do not get that love and support from the family, some give up the idea of getting married outside their religion while a few others go ahead and get married without family support. But this is a great source of stress, anxiety, agony and pain for the couple involved. Marriage in India is not an event but it is a lifelong relationship between husband and wife and between families. When such support is missing in the case of inter-religion marriages it can create and aggravate the social as well as psychological problems for the couple. The level of socio-psychological stress is often very high in such marriages and researches into this dimension will substantiate this point.

The chances are that over a period of time the husband's family will accept the bride but the wife's family finds it more difficult to accept the son-in-law who belongs to a different religious community. Our study reveals that in most cases where conversion had taken place the marriage was more easily acceptable to the husband's family. But, the girl's family often became more distanced from their daughter after the marriage of the daughter, especially if she was converted to Islam. In case of a registered marriage, the resentment from the husband's parents persisted over a longer period of time but the marriage was more acceptable to the parents of the bride. On the other hand as mentioned before, the parents of the boy agreed to the marriage and accepted it more readily if conversion of the girl had taken place. It is precisely to win the support of the boy's family with whom she had to live and interact for the rest of her life that conversion was seen as a way to adapt to the family of in-laws but the emotional price she has to pay for this is too much. Family support is, therefore, one of the main issues in inter-religion marriages. The children would be better adjusted and happier and contribute more to the composite culture and secular ethos of the society if their respective families and society at large were to support them. And, there would be many more of such marriages if parents and close relatives provided the necessary social support which they provide to marriages within the caste and within the religious community.

Conclusion

Marriage as an institution in India is considered to be most crucial for fortifying the religious adherence. It was not the union of man and woman for the purpose of procreation but the social association of two families. Consequently, to make the practice strict, society imposed numerous marital restrictions to enforce the traditional hierarchy of the caste system. Endogamy assured the identity and integrity of caste groups, family structure and the social system. Arranged marriages were considered to be a mechanism to preserve the caste hierarchy and restrict religious orientation. Marrying within one's own religion became the unsaid compulsory norm which was never to be challenged.

As Rao and Rao (1982: 111) observe, 'Marriages outside one's religious group are mainly exceptions. As a rule, people are expected to marry within their own religion. It was believed that due to cultural differences, marriages between persons of different religious backgrounds may not bring the expected adaptation on the part of the bride and bridegroom'. The pressures of tradition, obligation and expectation at various levels—family, community, and religion—such as 'consolidation of kin relationships, subjugation of individual interests to the family goals may not square with emphasis of other religious groups'.

Most religions either prohibit or discourage marriage between one of their devotees and someone of a different faith though India has been glorified for its multi-religious, multi-ethnic diversity and pluralistic characteristics. Yet mixed marriages are a rare occurrence. India has been following since time immemorial a rigid social structure that is based on the varna order, caste distinction. Daily rituals and strict practices have been providing a guideline for social acceptance, particularly, religion and caste marks the boundaries of social institutions like marriage. Deviation from the kin's decision and imposing self-choice and love-matches are looked upon with complete disapproval. A marriage of choice is frowned upon, and emphatically discouraged, and the pair is considered to be non-conforming.

It was always believed that marriages within the same faith reduce conflicts. Consequently, mixed marriages were not encouraged. For traditional societies, the perfect union of mind and full communion of life to which married couples aspired could be achieved only when both partners share the same belief and life. Mixed marriages involved constant adaptations on the part of the bride and groom. Despite all the restrictions, there are very few individuals who overcame the religiously prescribed norms of mate selection and married by choice. Yet young people, more recently, tend to select the 'right partner' they want to marry, with or without seeking the approval of their parents. The new generation became bolder in self-expression and decision-making. As a result, love marriages, specifically inter-religion marriages started figuring on the surface of Indian society. This study aims to understand, the challenges and ultimately, the fate of inter-religion marriages in a country like India, where religion, rituals and norms define the entire life of any individual.

It has been observed that inter-religion marriages find greater favour among socio-economic educated youth in urban areas. Most of these marriages take place in large cities, 'but even here they constitute a very small proportion' Shah (1998: 147), delineates the profile of parties in such marriages as upper caste, professional affluent and possessing higher educational degrees (often from overseas). The profile suggests a segment of the population who may not be subject to the pressures of conforming to traditional expectations, and who possess the socio-economic status to be more individualistic with regard to choices such as marriage partners. While there might be pressures from parents and immediate family, members of these groups are in a better position to exercise and realise personal and individual choice.

Inter-religion marriages are much less in number and largely an urban phenomenon. These are confined to the socio-economic elites of society. It is easier for elites to enter into an inter-religion marriage since traditional pressures of obligation to community may not be as strong as for members of other socio-economic backgrounds.

Inter-religion marriages show a value consensus that point out certain secular factors. Besides love being the most decisive factor of them in as much as it cuts across religious endogamy. In love marriages, whether inter-religion or not, the choice is made neither on physical attractiveness nor has status influenced the final choice of the mate. The character and personality of the partner has been essential for marriage. Regular factors like age, income, religion are not considered on priority. However compatibility between couples is reached if there are similar interests.

The size of the family, in terms of the number of siblings, parental education, or the pattern of socialisation has not materially influenced inter-marriage and had a minimal part in the selection of the spouse.

Another important factor which promotes inter-religion marriage is the occupational and education proximity of the partners. Bambwale (1982) points out that this is in contrast to the findings of the majority of American studies on love and marriage which brought out residential propinquity as the significant factor. She further states occupational propinquity reflected independent decisions taken by women who were wage earners. Thus we found that women, who move out of their homes, and were economically independent, can stand up against opposing factions essentially because of their status as breadwinners. Parents obviously have a greater hold over those children who are not financially independent.

In our sample of 50 couples in Delhi it was observed, the majority of girls are Hindu, who married Muslim boys. On the other hand, the percentage of Muslim girls getting married to Hindu boys is much less in number. The research shows that the reason for this disproportion seems to be the socialisation pattern of Muslim girls, who do not have enough exposure. Muslim society provides fewer opportunities to girls to interact with non-Muslim boys, whereas Hindu girls have greater exposure and more opportunities to interact with the opposite sex in educational institutions as well as in job situations. Also there is a feeling of greater loss to community when the Muslim girl gets married to a Hindu boy because Islam is a more closed system compared to Hinduism. The political history has been such that the Hindu-Muslim association has always been limited to the public sphere. Intrusion in the private sphere is strictly prohibited. Also, being a minority, the sense of insecurity is greater among Muslims, thus, any loss of membership in the community is looked upon as a greater loss.

Gender, more than community, seemed to influence the degree of parental and familial opposition, crossing community boundaries was viewed as an unpardonable offence unless the boy (a Hindu) is willing to convert to Islam. But, this rarely happens, because in a patriarchal society such as ours, adjustment to the boy's family is seen as the responsibility of the bride and in inter-religion marriages, this adjustment begins with conversion. There is also a sense of loss among the Hindus when a Hindu girl gets married to a Muslim boy, but the difference may be a matter of degree. In most cases where Hindu girls got married to Muslim boys it was almost taken for granted the girls would convert to Islam because Islam does not consider marriage as legitimate unless both the boy and girl are Muslims. Some girls accept Islam before marriage, others at the time of marriage and still others shortly after marriage. This process of conversion was also often seen as a facilitator in adjustments, adaptation and assimilation into the

Muslim communities. However, cases of conversions were witnessed specially where the couples lived in joint families and belonged to middle and lower middle class income groups.

In a few cases, the marriages were postponed for eight to ten years. Courtship was implicitly done secretly and the couple was in great strain due to opposition and condemnation of family and society, the individualistic actions of the duo involved in courtship was looked down upon, asperations were cast on the moral integrity of the couple. Parents and families were shocked and disagreed at the interviewees' decision to enter into inter-religious alliances. Consequently, 75 per cent of the respondents in our sample opted for court marriage, thus this further annoyed their parents and near and dear ones, the reason of their displeasure was the basis of the civil marriage and not secular beliefs.

Religion and social norms have always been the premier factor for successful existence in society. The idea of marrying outside a community threatened the rule as prescribed by the religious endogamy. Consequently, the opposition to inter-religion marriage came more because of fear of society than the fear of loss of faith. The pressure and punishment was not restricted to the couple but also to their siblings and sometimes to extended families. Their antagonism was not merely due to dissimilarity of religion but also because of apprehension of societal strain and difference in the social status and culture.

It must be noted that the civil weddings carry no traditional significance whatsoever among Indian communities, and parents and family would in no way consider it as an adequate substitute for a traditional community or customary wedding. Hence, even where all parties concerned had no opposition to the marriage and did not want either partner to convert, parents and family usually want a traditional wedding. This warranted nominal conversion on the part of one spouse (usually the woman). Although some gave significant attention to the notion of changing-religion, others were forced to convert by the spouse or the in-laws. In the personal laws that govern marriages for specific religious communities, there is no means by which parties of different religions can keep their religious identity while being married under any particular personal law. That is to say that a Hindu or Muslim marriage under their respective personal laws does not recognise the parties as at once Hindu and Muslim. Many interviewees faced problems because of the nature of the personal laws.

In fact, the majority of interviewees who underwent a nominal conversion did so because they could not participate in the ceremony while keeping their own religious identity. Compared to men, a large number of women changed their religion to their husband's religion; the conversion would mostly be by women only. The conversion was mostly under the pressure of in-laws or for the sake of the survival of the relationship. Children and their primary socialisation has also been a major reason for the conversion. The mother would not want the child to be confused about its religion. The majority of women followed the customs and rites of the religion they had converted into. There was significant religious freedom in celebration of the festivals. However there has been an attempt towards balancing between two cultures. The majority of the respondents did not have any problem in their children following the rituals of their spouse's religion and performed essential rites like naming ceremony, circumcision, etc. for their children.

Patterns of Adjustment

In inter-religion marriages, a considerable adjustment among the couples is of paramount importance. The efforts to achieve this harmony are through various stages of adaptation, reconciliation and assimilation. In the first step, the couple evolves into a stable relationship by reaching common conclusions which ultimately are suitable to both. Gradually these understandings are strongly visible in food habits, language, and celebration of festivals. The next stage of understanding is reached when a couple compromises about opinions including various issues which are beyond the behaviour adjustments. Amendment in the religious way of life was extremely complex with cultural differences at times accentuating the dissimilarities. Merely a small number of the married couples were beyond the notion of religious distinctiveness. Majority of the proportion of the investigated couples was found to be spiritually inclined. They expressed their religiosity in worshipping and celebrating the festivals of their personal religion. Even after the inter-religion marriage, the inter-religion married couples carried out rituals, went to temples, mosques as per their religious instructions, it was observed that more cultural space was available for the husband's religion.

The marital space is a gendered space, with unequal rights for men and women. India being a patriarchical society, most of the adjustments after the marriage are expected to be made by the women. So the major burden of adjustments in inter-religion marriages also falls on the women. But how well she is able to adjust depends to a great extent on the support that she receives from her husband, his family, and her own family, i.e. her parental family, friends, close relatives and the society in general. If the wife is also working which was true in most of the cases in such marriages, the attitude of the colleagues and employers is also a very important factor that helps the couple to adjust to each other, to the families and to the society. Autonomy, however, is contextually understood by women interviewees. Most of whom across class and community, report no diminution in autonomy after the marriage. Of the fifty couples interviewed there was only one case of divorce and that too not because of belonging to different religious communities but because of incompatibility.

Our study pointed out that the marital space is at once social and personal. The family and kinship has a greater impact before the marriage, when the decision to marry was announced, it led to opposition. Parental participation in the marriage ceremony paves the way for the postmarital reconciliation. The couple's future stand towards relatives and the possibilities of reconciliation and adjustment were determined by this factor.

When parents reconcile with their children a new area of interaction begins. The pattern of reconciliation points out that the greatest number of reconciliations took place after the marriage, while only a few had taken place before the marriage. The reconciliation of the parents with their son-in-law or daughter-in-law was found to be because the person was of good character, generous and understanding and helpful during difficulties. The emphasis again was on character as was seen in mate selection. This is a traditional value which has been retained in spite of the very modern pattern of mate selection and marriage. All in all, when we examine these interpersonal relationships and the comparative roles of the religious and the secular factor, we find that, their interaction is more important than each one's absolute importance. The religious factor is superimposed, however, on all the personal and inter-personal relationships. Thus we find that even after reconciliation with the couple, parents exclude many of these couples from rituals and rites in the parental homes. Further only a few of our respondents were welcome to visit their natal homes with their families. In some homes, they are welcomed with their children, but not with the spouse, and in yet other few homes only the respondents were allowed to visit their natal home. In India, a son-in-law is considered an important and esteemed guest in his father-in-law's home, but due to barriers of religion this is not possible in quite a number of cases of inter-religion marriages.This again is a part of the norms of purity and pollution, specially in the Hindu lifestyle.

Religious identity is critical in matters of marriage, in the imagination of the state as well as for the respective religious communities. Questions of religious identity would be the single most critical factor to be negotiated by the parties in an inter-religion marriage, even if the parties are not necessarily religious themselves. Given the polarisation between the majority and minority communities in India, inter-religion marriages of Muslims with Hindus especially would have to deal with the increasing communalisation of everyday life.

Couples in inter-religion marriages revealed various stages of the processes leading to marriage, and subsequent perceptions that each spouse belonged to communities that were primarily religious and essentially different. Their children too were often confronted with having to state their religious identity and 'prove themselves as of one religion or another'. It is the pressure of continually having to negotiate the prospect and consequences of social perceptions about being a Hindu or Muslim that recasts the act of an inter-religion marriage into something that is more than the choice of two individuals. In several cases, in fact, while individuals in inter-religion marriages see themselves as Hindu or Muslim, they do not consider their views, beliefs, or sense of self as exclusively dependent on the fact of belonging to a particular religious community. Nor do the interviewes perceive these categories in overwhelmingly religious terms. Yet individuals in such marriages have to face that in the imagination of society they are not perceived as two individuals married to each other, but as a Hindu married to a Muslim or a Muslim married to a Hindu. And that in this social imagination, Hindu and Muslim, and so on are designated as primarily religious categories.

Though the couple do not ascribe to the logic that they belong to different religions but the fact that others in society at large may well insist on viewing one according to one's place in such a framework, therefore negating whatever might be the individual's understanding about his or her identity, religion and religious difference. One is treated as a Hindu or Muslim, or a member of a particular religious group which have certain beliefs and customs.

This experience is not exclusively dependent on or specific to the situation of being in an inter-religion marriage, but as a result of such a marriage, one or both partners in the marriage are often exposed, in a sudden or direct manner, to these exclusive categories.

Uberoi (1993: 2) states that in Indian sociological literature, addressing the topic of marriage in India is an act fraught with anxiety. She further argues, 'It is as though a critical interrogation of the family might constitute an intrusion into that private domain where the nation's most cherished cultural values are nurtured and reproduced, as though the very fabric of society would be undone if the family were in any way questioned or reshaped'. What couples in inter-religion marriages and their children often encounter are precisely expressions of such social anxieties caused by the fact that the validity of an officially sanctioned socio-politico legal classificatory framework is called into question by the very act of inter-religion marriage and by the existence of children who are products of such marriages. What may produce the anxiety is that inter-religion marriages signify that religious identity may be much instrumental, performed, and a matter of choice and agency as it might be given predetermined or essential. While the partners in inter-religion marriages nearly inevitably have to negotiate given definitions and notions of religious identity and religious difference, it is the challenge that they represent to such notions of identity that often provokes a reaffirmation of those very structures of family. In this context, it should be mentioned that the couples interviewed for this study have challenged societal norms in a double sense, by entering into love marriages as well as inter-religion marriages.

Composite Culture and Inter-Religion Marriages

Secularism has different meanings and shades, in one sense it is 'viewed as a complete alternative and positive theory of life and conduct' of the individual and social life involving a complete rejection of any supernatural dimension in the sphere of human values, thought and actions. According to another interpretation, secularism means confining religion only to an individual's personal area of life and the complete disaffiliation of religion from other institutions including the state. The term secularisation implies that what was previously regarded as religion is now ceasing to be such, and it also implies a process of differentiation, which results in the various aspects of society, economic, political, legal and moral, becoming increasingly discreet in relation to each other'. With transition from simple to modern complex societies, we observe that individual choices have become more assertive. Though marriages are not only union of couples, they are also union of families and kinship. Inter-religion marriages act as a bridge in multicultural societies. Our case studies have shown by and large that it promotes understanding between the communities, and the community of mixed-heritage is very important to strengthen and promote the composite culture. The respondents have admitted that while considering the decision of inter-religion marriage, there was no intention to bring a social change. However, it cannot be denied that the secular upbringing of these respondents can be considered as an essential factor for their marriage. Yet, apart from the fact, whether change was consciously or unconsciously intended, it is undeniable that inter-religion marriages brought about social change in a very significant manner.

In spite of a large number of conversions, we have observed that a significant majority of couples celebrated all the festivals; participate in the auspicious and sad occasions in each other's household. Thus this interaction, though limited does act as an agent of change and as society is experiencing change. The social change in the institution of marriage is having an impact on the social structure. These kinds of marriages are more democratic and egalitarian. Higher education, allows interaction of different religious groups, to a great extent weakens the concept of religious endogamy in modern society. The very thought of crossing religious lines itself for the spouse, which was hitherto held in sacred trust as a family prerogative is a step towards the decreasing relevance of religion. They are unmistakably indicative of both modernisation and secularisation on one hand and on the other hand, they are themselves important contributory factors in the dissemination of these processes. The cumulative impact of this process would be the gradual emergence of a pluralistic society.

The children of mixed parentage grow up with liberal ideas

despite the religious orientation by the parents, the majority does not believe in bringing up children religiously. They show a remarkably liberal trend regarding their children's attitude towards religion. They felt that even though the children were initiated into a particular religion, since they had parents with a mixed religious background, the children should be allowed to opt for the religion of their preference when they attain adulthood. In theory the same principle of liberalism was observed in allowing freedom to children in choice of a mate. Respondents felt that their child's mate of any religion, even if different from that of the father or mother, was acceptable to them. Most interviewees indicate that decisions regarding their religious identities or children's identities are ultimately the concern of the couples.

However, few respondents reported intrusion of extended family into the personal marital space of the couple, but across the sample, individuals clearly distinguish the personal marital space from familial and social space.

Some of the couples spoke specifically on the topic of whether inter-religion marriages could or did contribute to inter-religious harmony and better relations among communities. Among those who spoke on the topic, the opinions are somewhat divided. Many felt that such marriages are a result of change in social attitudes. Some felt that such marriages if promoted and encouraged will strengthen the pluralistic traditions of the society and will give rise to a generation of more accepting people.

As stated before, mixed marriages were not intended for social change. However the study shows that these marriages were forms of deviance from the regular norms prescribed by society. Mixed marriages are considered to be modern in outlook. Despite being modern, marriage is viewed in a sacred context. The institution stays vulnerable to the changes in the religious sphere. One of our major findings is that, inter-religion marriages do not make religion irrelevant. A leaning towards secularism-meaning, thereby, a kind of disinterest and irrelevance about religion is envisaged as one possibility of development after inter-religious marriage. Reiss (1965), the American sociologist finds strong support for the hypothesis that inter-religious partners were less tied to their religion. This, however, is not concluded by the study. The persistence and continuity of religion is demonstrated in respect of its core features which indicate the vitality of the religious belief. Belief in God held by the respondents is obvious, for quite a few continue with daily worship, namaz, fasts and observing other rituals.

The desire for religious identity for various reasons is in existence and it has its own compulsions. This is manifested partially in conversion and in a slightly disguised form even in non-conversion. The religious identity of children is a matter of concern for the parents. In inter-religious marriages, love cuts across religious endogamy, rites and rituals seem to be abbreviated. The idea of purity and pollution is blurred. Further, visits to temples are also limited. Festivals seem to have retained their importance to some extent but with declining religious significance, their only importance as days of good will, good food, new clothes and merriment, meeting family and friends has acquired greater value. We can say that an interpersonal interaction start with the beginning of love and it continues through courtship and marriage.

A few areas of adjustment of the couple are more or less secular in nature. They cannot, however, be totally isolated from certain religious values, which creep in to influence the secular factors and vice versa. Language, sexual and temperamental areas of adjustment are totally secular and adjustment is quicker in these fields. Though food habits are adjustable with ease in some cases, one cannot ignore the fact that vegetarianism or non-vegetarianism are dependent on religious beliefs. As ideas or religious purity are ingrained by the process of socialisation, this particular factor may prove troublesome. Yet the respondents had solved this problem to their mutual satisfaction.

It is undeniable that marriage includes adjustments in order to be successful. The study has proved that these adjustments are secular and based on interpersonal relationships. After all, marriage involves togetherness and adjustment.

At the outset it must go on record that in response to questions in the interview, every respondent said that when they contemplated an inter-faith marriage, they did not have any conscious thought of bringing in any social change. Secularism as such was not their cherished goal. Yet, apart from the fact, whether change was consciously or unconsciously intended, it is undeniable that mixed inter-religious marriages are a phenomenon in the field of social change in a very significant manner. It is evident that they are not just individual or private arrangements. They are unmistakably indicative of both modernisation and secularisation on one hand. They are themselves important contributory factors in the dissemination of these processes. The cumulative impact of this process would be the slow emergence of a pluralistic society.

Looking Back: Reflection about Inter-Religion Marriages

As mentioned earlier, love has been a dominant factor in these marriages. Thus, this important feeling makes the marriage worthwhile. These years of relationship are supposed to bring in understanding and promote a feeling of togetherness and companionship even if it is full of all types of challenges.

The overwhelming majority of the couples in our study have stated that there are no regrets about marrying someone from another faith despite the opposition they faced for the life changing decision of marrying outside the religion. Growing as a couple has been an experience challenging their own perspective towards their own community and the other community. In fact the same sentiments are expressed by one of the respondents in another study on inter-religious marriage, conducted by Chopra and Punyani. The respondent questions his own "subconscious collectivism" as he describes it, 'my marriage taught me that it is essential to take a magnifying glass to one's own presumptions.' Even those who have faced hostility because of their being in inter-faith marriages have stood by their marriage. In spite of opposition, entrenchment of relationships of near and dear ones, it has been a journey of discovery of self and the other.

Couples do not in any way regret their decision to marry someone of another faith. However, many respondents also speak of the cost of the decision, there is pain where parents have cut off or limited their interaction and not accepted the marriage or spouse; there is a profound sense of being isolated as a minority among all religious communities; there is regret at what their children have had to go through and anxiety about what they may have to go through in the future. There is an awareness of the professional and social consequences of being in such a marriage.

Only two out of fifty couples regret the marriage, in one case (Hindu woman married to Muslim man), both partners regret marrying outside their community. While the wife says she regrets the marriage primarily because it has affected her children's marriage prospects, after her divorce she is unable to find brides for sons in the Hindu community, because the father of the sons is Muslim, after divorce also her sons are considered Muslims because of the patriarchal structure of society. In the second case (Muslim man-Hindu woman), it is only the husband who expresses regret at having married a Hindu; again, because of the social pressures they have had to face. Though his wife does not express regret, she does say, however, that she would not advise anyone to follow her example, 'they may not be as strong as I am. I've seen so many Hindu girls totally giving up their identity after marrying Muslims'. Her experience with her Muslim husband has been bitter, who has foisted his religion on her and has severely curtailed her freedom, and this has strongly prejudiced her opinion about Muslims.

There were a handful of interviewees who felt that inter-religious marriages contributed positively to inter-community relations, and were a step forward for society. Jasmeet felt 'we want people to know about us. They can see that such marriages can work too.' She says that her husband and sons, are one more family of the new type. Jasmeet and many more of our case studies were optimistic and felt that they are a new type of family, a bicultural family which will make all differences and hatreds disappear. Such marriages are something different, better and more tolerant.'

To conclude, the experiences of couples in inter-religion marriages reveal that it demands lot of courage to challange sociatal norms. Of course, couples from different religious backgrounds, married each other out of love and not to bring social change. Yet in challenging societal norms, and braving parental, familial, and societal opposition, the couples exemplify a significant process of social change. They stand as pillars of mutual respect, appreciation and integration between communities, and to the human experience of self-discovery and discovery of the other.

Future of Inter-Religious Marriages in India

There will probably be increase in inter-religion marriages between adherents of different religions across the world due to globalisation and migration of people. Both the processes facilitated by technological advances, have resulted in inevitable mixing of people of different religions and cultural traditions, the incidence and scope of inter-religion marriages will probably increase rather than decline.

Inter-religion marriages have always taken place in Indian society and will continue to take place. Hindu-Muslim marriages which are the most difficult of all inter-religion marriages have also taken place in the past, are taking place in contemporary society and will continue to take place in future. But the success of such marriages depends to a great extent on the couples, their adjustment pattern, their ability to face all odds, the support of the parents and the 'correct socialisation of their children', the support provided by the school and other educational institutions, neighbourhood, political environment and the secular values of society.

All marriages pass through different stages as they grow, couples grow together and discover each other while they traverse through this voyage, there are varied opinions on the success of mixed marriages, there are theories which say that it is difficult to adjust in heterogeneous marriages. The studies conducted in the West have tried to analyse the trend of divorce in mixed marriages, but in India we have a dearth of studies directly dealing with the question of success in inter-religion marriages, wherein we can analyse or claim that such marriages are prone to divorce. But the few studies conducted in India as mentioned earlier Abdullahi, Bambwale, Parvez Mody and our own study has indicated that though inter-religion marriages pass through rough terrain, face stress, strain due to cultural differences, opposition from the parents and society, yet there is low rate of divorce, the reason is a high sense of commitment and high respect for the institution of marriage. Divorce still is a stigma in our society. Our respondants have shared that the success of marriage is a compulsion to prove that their decision was not wrong. They understand that they will not be supported by parents/ relatives. This also happens as they have a long lasting and deep understanding with each other, the strong bonding emerging from overcoming all the hurdles together. This ensures that inter-religion marriages have a greater success rate.

In such marriages, where the individuals decide to marry without parents' approval, traditions like dowry and bride gifts do not become part of the wedding. These types of inter-religion marriages which are love marriages are based on mutual respect, the couples are more committed to stand by their commitment and responsibility. Since most of these marriages have taken place against the wish of the parents, last but not the least, the evil practice of dowry is also challenged through such marriages and there is hardly any claim of property by them. Therefore inter-religion marriages may be happening on a small scale but they are a very significant factor of inducing a positive social change in Indian society.

Undoubtedly those who marry inter-religiously follow an unconventional pattern and are prepared to accept the consequences of such a marriage. The need of the time is to accept such marriages and to provide the kind of support system that will make lives of such inter-religious couples and their children more comfortable and less taxing so that they can contribute to the secular ethos of our society and create an environment of freedom, love and respect for human beings. The anguish of the couples and the children can be summed up in a few sentences thus, 'we would expect our society to be more supportive of such marriages so that our children can live with dignity and harmony in society with fearlessness. They may be alienated socially and emotionally because of the inter-religion marriage of their parents. Let us provide them with such an environment wherein they can live, grow and develop with dignity and a sense of pride. Inter-religion marriages compared to intra-religious marriages have many positive attributes especially in Indian society where issues of castes, communalism and regionalism have divided people.

Inter-religion marriages are a small but a very significant step in the direction of bridging the gap between the communities which in some cases are considered oppositely positioned in the society. It promotes multiculturalism and pluralism. These couples and their children act as agents of social change inducing religious tolerance. The pluralistic situation is one in which different beliefs and values coexist, these marriages are a very big step in the direction of removing the prejudices against different communities caused by stereotypes of the communities, which in turn encourages better understanding, and therefore resulting in greater religious tolerance leading to more social harmony by strengthening the pluralistic traditions and promoting secularisation.

Indeed secularisation and pluralism may be said to be in a dialectical relationship, they reciprocally reinforce one another. Secularisation produces pluralism by weakening the religious monopoly that at one time had dominated most societies. From this perspective, one can envisage a dialectical relationship between inter-religious marriages and inter-communal relations, whereby what happens at one level is likely to affect the other. It would therefore seem to follow that the formulation and implementation of well-informed and enlightened social policy in such settings is critical not only for the material and moral well-being of the spouses and children of inter-religion marriages, but also for better inter-communal relations in general.

While this three generation study will be interesting and useful for the scholarly understanding of the relationship between religions, family and community in general, it is also hoped that the outcome will be helpful for policy makers and community leaders in different parts of the world regarding issues of inter-religion marriages in particular. A clearer understanding of the social realities of these marriages for spouses, their parents and children in their respective communities is necessary not only for addressing the needs and concerns of directly affected parties, but also for enhancing the prospects of mutual respect and harmony among different religious communities.

It is no accident that for centuries, the world over, parents and older relatives have controlled or supervised the selection of mates for their sons and daughters. Certainly their counsel, in such undertakings as an inter-religious marriage, should be taken into account. Whatever the possibilities of happiness in mixed marriages, the path to them must always be through the areas of understanding, tolerance, compromise and mutual respect. Family happiness is not an accident, nor a gift, nor an incident. It does not come by legislative fiat, priestly blessing, or as a result of the ordering and forbidding technique. It is not created by sermons from pulpits or denouncements in the daily press. From these and other sources may come counsel and guidance, inspiration and suggestion, but at best these are threads which each family can weave into its own fabric as the loom of its daily life shuttles back and forth in the continuing give-and-take of group living.

Family happiness is an achievement. It results from intelligent and cooperative effort. Families are happy because they work at it, because they seek consciously and sensibly to promote happiness. The slogan of religious groups that 'families that pray together, stay together' might be restated to say that families that can do things together plan things together, share and enjoy things together, stay together. The key word is "together".

It is against this background that mixed marriages, in the final analysis, must be considered. Once consummated, whatever the difficulties, with these as with life's other burdens, one must carry them, and move on. And they should be carried, not with the breaking ache of bitterness or the impediment of a crippling paralysis, but in one's stride as responsibilities which have been assumed, after all, in the freedom of adult choice.Moreover the conditions of multiculturism, cultural pluralism and globalisation that make inter-religion marriages more likely in the near future than it is now emphasise the importance of peaceful co- existence and genuine acceptance of religious and cultural differences. Given the critical role of family and community in the formation and development of social and legal institutions, inter-religion marriages are a useful prism for understanding relations, between different religious traditions.

Bibliography

Anderson, Robert N, and Rogelio Saenz. "Structural Determinants of Mexican American Inter-marriage 1975-1980." *Social Science Quarterly* 75 (1994): 37-52.

An-Na'im, Abdullahi. *Inter-Religious Marriage Among Muslims: Negotiating Religious and Social Identity in Family and Community.* New Delhi: Global Media Publications, 2005.

Bambawale, Usha and A. Ramanamraa. "Mate Selection in Inter-Religious Marriages; an Indian Perspective." *Indian Journal of Social Work* 42(2) (1981): 165-173.

Bambawale, Usha. *Inter-religious Marriages.* Pune: Dastane Ramchandra and Co., 1982.

Barnett, Larry D. "Inter-racial Marriages in California." *Marriage and Family Living*, 1963: 424-427.

Barot, J. *Modern trends in Marital Relation: The Indian Family in the Change and Challenge of The Seventies.* New Delhi: Sterling Publishers, 1972.

Besanceney, Paul H. *Inter-faith Marriages: Who and Why.* New Haven: College and University Press, 1970.

Blood, Robert O,. *The Husband and Wife Relationship.* Chap XX in Edited by F. lvan Nye and Lois W Hoffman. Chicago: Rand-McNally, 1963.

Botev, N. "Where East Meets West: Ethnic Inter-marriage in the Former Yugoslavia 1962 to 1989." *American Sociological Review* 59 (1994): 461-80.

Bourdieu, Pierre. "Marriage Strategies of Social Reproduction." Edited by R. Forster and O. Ranum. *In Family and Society*, Johns Hopkins University Press, 1976.

Burchinal, L. G et Chanceixor, L.E. "Survival Rates Among Religiously

Homogamous and Interreligious Marriages." *Social Forces* 41 (1963): 353-362.

Burgess, E. and P. Wallin. "Homogamy in Social Characteristics." *American Journal of Sociology* 49 (1943): 109-24.

Burgess, E.W. and L. S. Cottrell. *Predicting Success of Failure in Marriage.* New York: Prentice-Hall, 1939.

Burgess, E.W. and P. Wallin. "Homogamy in Social Characteristics." *American Journal of Sociology* 49 (1943): 109-124.

Burgess E.W. and Locke H.J. *The Family: From Institution to Companionship.* 2nd Edition. New York: American Book Co., 1953.

Cerroni-Long, E.L. "Marrying Out: Socio-Cultural and Psychological Implications of Inter-marriages." Edited by G. Kurian. *Journal of Comparative Family Studies* 16(1) (1985): 25-46.

Chatterjee, Partha. *Secularism and Tolerance.* In *Secularism and its Critics.* Edited by Rajeev Bhargava. New Delhi: Oxford University Press, 1998.

Chatterjee, Partha. *The Nation and its Fragments: Colonial & Postcolonial Histories.* Oxford University Press, 1993.

Chinitz, J.G., and R.A. Brown. "Religious Homogamy, Marital Conflict and Stability in Same-Faith and Inter-faith Jewish Marriage". *Journal for the Scientific Study of Religion* 40 (2001): 723-33.

Corwin, Lauren A. "Caste, Class and The Love-Marriage: Social Change in India." *Journal of Marriage and the Family* 39(4) (1977): 823-31.

Cott, Nancy. *Public Vows: A History of Marriage and the Nation.* Cambridge, Mass: Harvard University Press, 2000.

Crester, G., and J.J. Leon. "Inter-marriage in The US: An Overview of Theory and Research." *Marriage and Family Review* 5 (1982): 3-15.

Datta, Pati B., S. Sarkar, T. Sarkar, S. Sen. "Understanding Communal Violence: Nizamuddin Riots." *Economic and Political Weekly*, Nov. 1990: 2487-95.

Davidson, James, and Tracy Widman. "The Effects of Group Size on Inter-faith Marriage Among Catholics." *Journal for the Scientific Study of Religion* 41, no. 3 (2002): 397-404.

Davis, K. "Inter-marriage in Caste Societies." *American Anthropologist* 43 (1941): 388-95.

Deshpande, C.G., *A Comparative Study of Caste and Intercaste Marriages (Unpublished).* Pune: Pune University, 1969.

Deutsch, Karl. "Social Mobilization and Political Development." *American Political Sceince Review* 55(3), 1961: 493-514.

Ellman, Y. "Inter-marriage in the United States: A Comparative Study of Jews and Other Ethnic Groups." *Jewish Social Studies* 49 (1987): 1-26.

Ellen Jaffe-Gill, Ellen Jaffe McClain. *Embracing the strangers: Intermarriage and the future of the American Jewish Community.* Basic Books Publication, 1995.

Firth, Raymond, *Dynamics of Culture Change (1945) in Man and Culture: An Evalution of the Work of Bronislaw Malinowski.* London: Routledge and Kegan Paul, 1963.

Fox, Robin. *Kinship and Marriage: An Anthropological Perspective.* Middlesex: Penguin, 1967.

Fu, Xuanning. "Interracial Marriage and Status Exchange: A Study of Pacific Islanders in Hawaii from 1983 to 1994." *Pacific Studies* 22, No. 1 (1999): 51-75.

Ghurye, G.S., "Social Change in Maharashtra." *Sociological Bulletin* 1 (1952): 71-88.

G.M. Speelman. *Keeping faith: Muslim-Christian couples and interreligious dialogue.* Meinema, 2001.

Glaser, Gabrielle. *Stranger to the Tribe: Portraits of Inter-faith Marriage.* Houghton Mifflin, 1997.

Giddens, Anthony. *The Transformation of Intimacy: Sexuality, Love and Eroticism in Modern Societies.* Cambridge: Polity Press, 1992.

Glick, P.C. and Carter, H. "Marriage Patterns and Educational Level." *American Sociological Review* 23(3) (1958): 294-300.

Goode, W.J. "The Theoretical Importance of Love." *American Sociological Review* 24 (1959): 38-47.

Gordon, Albert I. *Inter-marriage: Inter-Faith, Inter-Racial Inter-Ethnic.* Boston: Greenwood Publishing Group Press, 1980

Gore, M.S. *Urbanization and Family Change.* Bombay: Popular Prakashan, 1968.

Goswami, K.G. *Inter caste Marriage in Ancient India.* Calcutta: Sanskrit Pustak Bhandar, 1972.

Gupta, Charu. "(Im)possible Love and Sexual Pleasure in Late Colonial North India." *Modern Asian Studies* 36(1) (2002): 195-221.

Harlan, Lindsey and Paul B. Courtright. Introduction: *On Hindu Marriage and Its Margins.* New York: Oxford University Press, 1995.

Heer, D.M. "Trends of Inter-faith Marriages in Canada 1922-1957." *American Sociological Review* 27 (1962): 245-250.

Heer, David. "The Prevalence of Black-White Marriage in the US, 1960 and 1970." *Journal of Marriage and the Family* 36 (1974): 246-58.

Hirschmann Charles. "America's Melting Pot Reconsidered." *Annual Review of Sociology* 9 (1983): 397-423.

Hoge, Dean R. "Sociological Research on Inter-faith Marriage in America." *The Greek Orthodox Theological Review* 40, no. 3-4 (1995): 299-312.

Hunt, Chester, and Co Her, R.W. "Inter-marriage and Cultural Change: A Study of Philippine-American Marriage." *Social Forces* 35 (1957): 223-230.

Hwang, S.S, Saenz, R. and Aquirre, B.E. "Structural and Assimilationist Explanations of Asian American Inter-marriage." *Journal of Marriage and The Family* , 1997: 758-772.

Hwant et. al., "Structural and Assimilationist Explanations of Asian American Inter-marriage." *Journal of Marriage and the Family* 59 (1997): 758-72.

J.H. Newell. "Inter-Caste Marriage in Kugti Village, Himachal Pradesh in India". *Man*, 59/60, 1963: 55-57.

Jacobs, Jerry A. and Teresa G. Labov. "Gender Differentials in Inter-marriage Among Sixteen Race and Ethnic Groups." *Sociological Forum* 17, no. 4 (2002): 621-46.

John, Lievens. "Interethnic Marriage: Bringing in the Context through Multilevel Modelling." *European Journal of Population/Revue Europeenne de Demographic* 14, no. 2 (1998).

John L. Thomas. "The Factor of Religion in the Selection of Marriage Mates" *American Sociological Review* 16 (1951) 487-491.

Kakar, Sudhir and John M. Ross. *Tales of Love, Sex and Danger.* New Delhi: Oxford University Press, 1995.

Kannan, C.T. *Inter-caste and Inter-community Marriage in India.* Bombay: Allied Publishers, 1963.

Kaplan, Jane. *Inter-faith Families: Personal Stories of Jewish-Christian and Jews.* Church Publishing Incorporated, 2005.

Kapadia, K.M. *Marriage and Family in India.* Calcutta: Oxford University Press, 1988.

Kaur, Ravinder. "Across-Region Marriages: Poverty, Female Migration and the Sex Ratio." *Economic and Politicaly Weekly* 39, no. 25 (2004): 2595-603.

Kerckhoff, A.C. and Davis E.E. "Value Consensus and Need Complementarity in Mate Selection." *American Sociological Review* 27, no. 3 (1962): 295-303.

Klemer, Richard H. *Marriage and Family Relationship.* Harper and Row, 1970.

Ktsanes, T. "Mate Selection on the Basis of Personality Type: A Study Utilising Empirical Typology of Personality." *American Sociological Review* 20 (1955): 546-551.

Kulczycki, Andrzej, Arun Peter Lobo. "Patterns, Determinants and

Implications of Inter-marriage Among Arab Americans." *Journal and Marriage and Family* 64 (2002): 202-210.

Landis, J.T. and Landis, M.G. *Building a Successful Marriage*, 4th Edition. Englewood Cliffs N J: Prentice Hall, 1963.

Lantz, H. R and Snyder E. C. *Marriage: An Examination of the Man-Woman relationship*. New York: John Wiley and Sons, 1969.

Larsson, Clotye Murdock. *Marriage Across The Colour Line*. Johnson Publisher Co., 1965.

Lateef, Shahida. *Muslim Women in India: Political and Private Realities 1890s-1980s*. New Delhi: Kali for Women, 1990.

Leary, Richard O. "Change in the Rate and Pattern of Religious Inter-marriage in the Republic of Ireland." *The Economic and Social Review* 30, no. 2 (1999): 119-132.

Lehrer, Evelyn L. "The Role of Religion in Union Formation: An Economic Perspective." *Population Research and Policy Review* 23(2) (2004).

Levi-Strauss, Claude. *Elementary Structures of Kinship*, translated by James H. Bell, John R. von Sturmer and Rodney Needham. Boston: Beacon Press, 1969.

Liang, Zia, and Naomi Ito. "Inter-marriage of Asian Americans in the New York City Region: Contemporary Patterns and Future Pospects." *International Migration Review* 33, no. 4 (1999).

Lopata, H.Z. *Marriage and Families: A Transaction, Society Reader*. New York: D. Van Nostrand, 1973.

Lowie, Robert. *Primitive Religion*. New York: G. Routledge and Sons Limited, 1925.

Luhmann, Niklas. *Love as Passion: The Codification of Intimacy*. Cambridge: Polity Press, 1986.

Macfarlane, Alan. *Marriage and Love in England: Modes of Reproduction*. Oxford: Basil Blackwell, 1986.

Mahmood, Tahir. *Civil Marriage Law Perspectives and Prospects*. New Delhi: Indian Law Institute, 1978.

Mayer, Egon. *Love and Tradition: Marriage between Jews and Christians*. New York, 1985.

McClain, E. J. *Embracing The Stranger: Inter-marriage and The Future of The American Jewish Community*. New York: Basic Books, 1995.

Merton, Robert. "Inter-marriage and the Social Structure: Fact and Theory" in the *Blending American: Patterns of Inter-marriage*. Edited by Milton L Barron. Chicago: Quadrangle Books, 1941.

Mittal, L.N. "Gandhi and Hindu-Muslim Marriages." *Economic and Political Weekly* 34, no. 50 (1999): 11-17.

Mody, Perveez. "Kidnapping, Elopement and Abduction: An

Ethnography of Love-Marriage in Delhi." Edited by F. Orsini. *Love in South Asia: A Cultural History*. Cambridge University Press, 2006: 331-44.

________. "Love and The Law: Love-Marriage in Delhi." *Modern Asian Studies* 36, no. 1 (2002): 223-56.

________. *The Intimate State: Love-Marriage and The Law in Delhi*. New Delhi: Routledge, 2008.

Mokashi, P.R. *Some Social Aspects of Marriage in Poona District 1995-56.* Poona: Poona University, 1965.

Monahan, Thomas. "Some Dimensions of Interreligious Marriages in Indiana1962-1967." *Social Forces* 52 (1973): 195-203.

Mustick, Marc, and John Wilson. "Religious Switching for Marriage Reasons." *Sociology of Religion* 6 (1995): 257-70.

Nelson, L. "Inter-marriage Among Nationality Groups in a Rural Area of Minnesota." *American Journal of Sociology* 48, no. 5 (1943): 585-592.

Nimkoff, Meyer Francis. *Marriage and the Family*. Houghton Mifflin Co. 1947.

Parashar, Archana. *Women and Family Law Reforms in India: Uniform Civil Code and Gender Equality*. New Delhi: Sage Publications, 1992.

Park, Robert E. *Race and Culture.* Clencoe, IL: Free, 1950.

Pike, James Albert. *If you marry outside your faith: Counsel on Mixed Marriages.* Harper Publisher, 1954.

Peach, C. "Which Triple Melting Pot? A Re-Examination of Ethnic Inter-marriage in New Haven." *Ethnic and Racial Studies* 3, no. 1 (1980): 1-16.

Philips, B.A. *Re-Examining Inter-marriage: Trends, Textures and Strategies.* Los Angeles, CA: the Wilstein Institute of Jewish Policy Studies and The American Jewish Committee, 1997.

Punwani and Chopra. "Discovering the Other, Discovering the Self: Inter-Religious Marriage Among Muslims" in the Greater Bombay Area, India. In *Inter-Religious Marriages Among Muslims.* Edited by Abdullahi A. An-Na'im. New Delhi: Global Media Publications, 2005.

Punwani, Jyoti. *"The Carnage at Godhra."* In *Gujarat: the Making of a Tragedy*. Edited by Siddarth Varadarajan. New Delhi: Penguin, 2002.

Qureshi, M. Hashim. *Introduction. In Muslims in India Since Independence. A Regional Perspective.* New Delhi: Institute of Objective Studies, 1998.

Rao, V.V. Prakasha and Nandini Rao. *Marriage, The Family and Women in India.* New Delhi: Heritage Publishers, 1982.

Reiss, Ira. *Love and Mate Selection: Reading on the Family System.* New York: Holt Rinehart and Wintson, 1972.

Reiss, Paul J. "The Trend in Inter-faith Marriage." *Journal for the Scientific Study of Religion* 5 (1965): 64-67.

Roberts, B. *Biographical Research.* Buckingham: Open University Press, 2002.

Rodrigues, Melba Marie. *A Comparative Study Between Inter and Intra Religious Married Couples.* Delhi: University of Delhi (Unpublished), 1990.

Rose, Anne C. *Beloved Strangers: Inter-faith Families in Ninteenth Century America.* Harvard University Press, 1950.

Rosenbaum, Mary Helene Rosenbaum and Stanley Ned. *Celebrating our Differences: Living Two Faith in One Marriage.* Ragged Edge Press, 1994.

Rubin, Z. "Do American Women Marry Up?" *American Sociological Review* 33 (1968): 750-760.

Sanghvi, L.D. "Inbreeding in India." *Social Biology* 29, no. 1-2 (1982).

Schneider, Susan Weidman. *Inter-marriages: The Challenges of Living with Differences between Christian and Jews.* Free Press, 1989.

Sen, Amartya. Secularism and its Discontents. In *Secularism and Its Critics.* New Delhi: Oxford University Press, 1998.

Shah, A.M. *The Family in India: Critical Essays.* New Delhi: Orient Longman, 1998.

Shorter, Edward. *The Making of the Modern Family.* Fontana: Glasgow: Collins and Fontana Press, 1977.

Sikand, Yoginder. "Islam and Caste Inequality Among Indian Muslims". Qalandar, March 2004 issue, http://www.islaminter-faith.org/mar2004/ issue-03-04, html

Sinha, R.K. et al. *Marriage in India: Contours, Correlates and Consequences.* Bombay: Himalaya Publishing House, 1999.

Speelman, G.M. *Keeping Faith: Muslim-Christian Couples and Inter-Religious Dialouge.* Zoetermeer, The Netherlands: Meinema, 2001.

Srinivas, M.N. *Caste in Modern India and Other Essays* . Bombay: Asia Publishing House, 1962.

Subba Rao, G.C.V. *Family Law in India.* 7th Edition. New Delhi: Gogia Publishers, 1998.

Sundal, P.A. and T. McCormick. "Age at Marriage and Mate Selection, Madison, Wisconsin 1937-1943." *American Sociological Review* 16 (1951): 37-48.

Thomas, John L.. "The Factor of Religion in the Selection of Marriage Mates". *American Sociological Review* 16 (1951), 487-491.

Tucker, M.B. and C. Mitchell-Kernan (Eds.). *The Decline of Marriage*

Among African American Causes Consequences, and Policy Implications. New York: Russell Sage Foundation, 1995.

Uberoi, Patricia. "Regional Varieties: North and South." Edited by Patricia Uberoi. In *Family, Kinship and Marriage in India.* (Oxford University Press), 1993: 45-49.

Westermarck, Edward. *The History of Human Marriage.* 5th Edition. New York: Macmillan, 1921.

Williamson, R.C. *Marriage and Family Relations.* USA: John Wiley, 1966.

Wilson, B R. "Morality in The Evolution of the Modern Social System." *British Journal of Sociology* 36 (1985): 315-32.

Winch, R.F. "A Theory of Complementary Needs in Mate Selection: A Test of One kind of Complementariness." *American Sociological Review* 20 (1955): 52-56.

Yancey, George. "Who Inter-racially Dates: An Examination of The Characteristics of Those Who Have Inter-racially Dated." *Journal of Comparative Family Studies* 33, no. 2 (2002): 179-90.